SHOTS FIRED

SHOTS FIRED

The Psychology Behind Officer Involved Shootings

CHUCK J. RYLANT

ISBN-10: 0-9839637-4-6

ISBN-13: 978-0-9839637-4-5

Published by:

Perfect Life Publishing
793 Foothill Boulevard, Suite 165
San Luis Obispo, CA 93405-1683

Cover and Interior Design:

Jerry & Michelle Dorris
Authorsupport.com

BEFORE YOU CONTINUE

As a reader of this book, you are entitled to FREE additional interviews and updates.

As a FREE registered VIP member at www.ChuckRylant.com, you will receive brand-new interviews and other inspiring articles immediately as they are published.

Visit www.ChuckRylant.com and join the VIP list before you get distracted.

Each of these 12 stories are first hand, true accounts of the shootings told directly by each officer. A few of the officer's names have been changed by request.

CONTENTS

INTRODUCTION

Antipolice media propaganda has deceived the public and turned decent citizens against the police officers who risk their lives to protect them.

The media narrative about officer-involved shootings is very different from the reality. Typical racist headlines like "White Cop Shoots Black Man" are often the only exposure law-abiding citizens have to police officers.

Most people have never been in a physical fight, let alone a life-or-death shooting, so they are left with Hollywood and media fiction to *educate* them about law enforcement shootings.

The perception is that cops are cavalier about shooting people, but from the 12 real-life accounts in this book, you will discover law enforcement shootings are far more complicated and the consequences are greater than most people will ever understand.

Each fascinating chapter in this book illustrates how shootings occur under intense pressure, with limited information, and in rapidly evolving situations.

Law enforcement demands a tough exterior, but officer-involved shootings are extremely traumatic. Officers risk not only being killed but also imprisonment, loss of employment, public slander, marriage and family turmoil, and severe health issues.

The psychology behind an officer-involved shooting is the part of the story that is missing from the public narrative. What happens in the officer's head before, during, and after a shooting is the story that is rarely told.

Police officers, like all humans, make less-than-perfect decisions and occasionally stumble with significant mistakes. That said, in virtually every law enforcement shooting, the suspect's actions drive the officer to shoot—it is not the other way around.

This book is for three kinds of people:

1. Cops who have been in a shooting
2. Cops who could be in a shooting
3. Civilians who want to understand police shootings

Law enforcement culture penalizes officers for showing vulnerability, so it can be easy to feel alone when experiencing the trauma that follows killing another human. This book shares the story that officers do not get to tell, and it will prepare others who have not yet been forced to pull the trigger.

ADAM RAMOS

"It's that sixth sense, man," Adam Ramos said. "It didn't feel right, and I felt like something bad was going to happen."

Adam was part of the narcotics team planning to arrest a drug dealer who carried a gun and boasted about killing cops.

The narcs requested the SWAT team, but the bureaucrats forced them to come up with another plan to save money on overtime expenses. The alternative was to catch the dealer in his car instead of raiding the house.

"I wasn't comfortable with it," Adam said. "I knew this guy was dangerous, and it didn't feel right."

Adam sat in an undercover car, waiting for the suspect to leave his house, and when the dealer drove off, Adam called it in to his partners. They were standing by around the corner in two unmarked police vehicles.

At a stop sign, the officers tried to box in the drug dealer's car with a van in front and an SUV behind.

"It wasn't tight enough," Adam said. "He saw it coming and broke out."

The drug dealer accelerated, and the officers chased him in their unmarked vehicles. After a brief pursuit, the dealer wrecked his Suburban outside his own house.

Adam was driving the third car in the pursuit, and after the Suburban crashed, Adam ran toward the door on the driver's side, where his partners were already fighting with the suspect.

"Gun, gun, gun," an officer yelled. "He's got a fucking gun."

Adam heard the sound of gunfire, but the shots were not as loud as he was used to hearing on the shooting range.

"Shit, I'm going to get shot," Adam feared as he was running to get into the fight.

Another officer stood in front of the Suburban, shooting at the drug dealer through the windshield.

Adam had been working undercover surveillance, so he was not wearing a bulletproof vest. He abruptly turned and ran toward the passenger side of the Suburban to use it as cover.

"That's when I ran into the passenger," Adam said. "He wasn't going with the program because he was watching his uncle get shot. I threw him to the ground, and we started fighting."

Adam looked up from his own fight and saw an officer lying on his back, holding the drug dealer in a choke hold.

"There was shooting going on everywhere," Adam said. "I was fighting with this guy, and I looked over and I'm watching all this shit go down. It was nuts."

Adam finally got the passenger in handcuffs and looked up and saw that his partners were still fighting at the door on the driver's side.

"That's when another officer put a .45 to [the dealer's] head and pulled the trigger," Adam said.

The suspect immediately went limp with a gun in his hand and an officer lying underneath him.

In the immediate lull of the fight, Adam noticed that the officer holding the suspect had been shot through his hands.

"I started wrapping his hands with gauze from an emergency kit," Adam said. "I looked up and another officer was lying in a puddle of blood, with his vest ripped open."

"That's when this fucking mess really hit me," Adam said. "We were close and coached our daughters' soccer team together. Now I'm going to have to tell his wife that he's dead."

The entire incident lasted seconds, and when it was over, an officer reported, "Shots fired, officer down," over the radio.

"That's when the cavalry came with lights and sirens blaring," Adam said. "Even the police chief showed up."

They needed to clear the dealer's house, so Adam strapped on his vest and took a position covering the southeast corner.

"I was scared on the perimeter," Adam said. "All these things ran through my mind, and that's when the anxiety started coming on. I didn't know if my friend was dead, and I felt like my heart was racing out of my chest. I was freaking out."

While guarding the perimeter with his gun drawn, Adam remembered it was his wife's birthday and they were supposed to go out to dinner that night.

"This is a mess," Adam thought. "I gotta call my wife."

Officers threw flash-bang grenades, stormed the house, and handcuffed everyone inside.

It was the first shooting incident Adam had ever experienced, so after everything calmed down he sat on the curb, shivering in the cold and waiting to see what would come next.

"What the fuck happened?" Adam wondered as he sat trying to process everything. "It happened so fast. What went wrong?"

Adam remembered police academy instructors teaching him to visualize high-risk scenarios while driving around on patrol.

"I'd run scenarios through my head before, but never once did I think of a scenario of my partner getting shot," Adam said. "I wasn't prepared for that at all."

Adam experienced a bit of survivor's guilt and questioned what he could have done differently to prevent his partner from getting shot.

"I'm the idiot that wasn't wearing a vest," Adam said. "Just by Murphy's Law, I should've taken a round, but I'm walking out unscathed."

Later that day, Adam visited the injured officer at the hospital and learned that his injury was not life threatening.

Adam was trying to make it to his wife's birthday dinner, so he was the first to be interviewed.

"Legal defense does not cover you as a witness," the police attorney told Adam, "but I don't trust your administration, so I'm going in there with you anyway."

Adam said it was easy to remember the incident during the interview, but days later he recalled details he did not initially remember.

"It was like watching a movie with missing clips," Adam said. "And then watching it again, going, 'Oh shit, I didn't see that part.'"

It was not until days later that Adam remembered seeing one of the officers raise his rifle and take the shot that accidently hit the officer Adam thought had been killed.

The night of the accident, Adam went home and took a shower before his wife's birthday dinner.

"I remember closing my eyes to wash my hair and having a flashback," Adam said. "As clear as in a movie, I saw the officer put a gun to [the dealer's] head and shoot. He went limp and his face turned gray. He went from life to death in that second."

When Adam got to the dinner party, he started drinking heavily.

"I remember looking back at pictures of that family dinner and I'm like a zombie," Adam said. "I'm looking out in the middle of nowhere and I'm not even there."

4

When Adam and his wife got home, his wife wanted to know what happened.

"We've been married long enough," Adam said. "She can tell when I'm sugarcoating something, so I told her everything."

She was very supportive and told Adam, "That guy chose his actions, and that's why he's dead. I'm just glad you're home with me and the kids."

Before they went to bed, she wanted to watch the news to see what the suspect looked like.

"I was drunk and falling asleep," Adam said. "But I remember her listening to the news and saying, 'This is crazy.'"

The police commander told Adam that he could not take any time off because Adam was not one of the shooters. He was back to work at 7:00 AM the next day.

"I thought he approached it wrong," Adam said. "He should have asked how we felt and offered us some vacation time to decompress."

About a week later, one of the maintenance guys at work walked up and asked Adam about the shooting. He was the first person to mention the shooting since it happened.

"I started sweating and my heart started racing like it was going to come out of my chest," Adam said. "I told him to get away from me. I wanted to hit him."

Adam left the station and started driving around, but the feeling was not going away. He started feeling numbness in his fingers, and his arms were tingling. Adam drove himself to the emergency room, where they hooked him up to a bunch of monitors.

"Your vitals are normal," the doctor said.

"Dude, something's wrong," Adam said. "Hook me back up to that machine, because something's not right."

The doctor said Adam was having an anxiety attack, so he prescribed something to help Adam sleep.

"I was scared to ask for help," Adam said. "But at the hospital, I finally told my sergeant that something was wrong. I thought for sure he was going to say 'You're just a pussy.'"

"I started freaking out," Adam said. "They're going to think I'm crazy and take my gun. I'm going to lose my fucking job, and I'm not going to be able to support my family. All of those thoughts added to my fear."

Fortunately, the administrators surprised Adam by being supportive. They offered him some time off to see a doctor and waited for her recommendations.

"Had they taken my gun that day, I would have completely freaked out," Adam said. "That's like taking a hammer from a carpenter. How's he supposed to support his family? It's a whole mental thing that you're thinking you're no longer a cop."

Adam was not able to sleep that night and kept waking up in a cold sweat. The next day, Adam's wife drove him to the psychologist.

"I couldn't even drive," Adam said. "That's how freaked out I was. I thought I was going fucking nuts."

The psychologist explained that his feelings were normal for someone who'd experienced a traumatic situation, and she assured him he would be fine. She wanted Adam to take time off but encouraged him to keep busy.

"Part of anxiety is to sit and constantly worry," the psychologist told Adam. "She told me it's a trigger from the back part of your brain that never shuts off, [so it constantly] produces anxiety."

That professional reassurance helped calm Adam's nerves, but for about a month he lost his appetite.

"I lost 13 pounds in nine days," Adam said. "I'd wake up in the middle of the night, having to use the restroom, because my stomach was all jacked up. I had black circles under my eyes, and I looked like death. It was rough, man."

Every evening, Adam became extremely emotional, so he slept at his parents' house.

"I was so concerned about my kids seeing me go through this," Adam said. "As soon as it got dark, the pressure hit me and I started crying for no reason whatsoever. I couldn't help it. I'd never been through anything like this before. It was scary."

The doctor prescribed Adam an antidepressant that worked very well for a couple of months.

"That helped, but it also hurt," Adam said. "I wasn't depressed or anxious anymore, but it gave me a carefree attitude. I didn't care about anything, and that caused some huge problems in my marriage."

In hindsight, Adam believed his dosage was too high.

"I was doing a lot of stupid shit," Adam said. "I was staying out late drinking at the bars and getting careless because I didn't sweat the small things."

"I pushed my wife away," Adam said. "I pushed the one person away who was there for me the whole time because she was calling me on my bullshit."

While he was growing distant from his wife, his relationship with his children grew closer.

"I realized how quickly death happens," Adam said. "I wanted to be closer to my kids."

After Adam had taken about three months away from work, the emotions from the shooting began to fade away. The doctor took him off his medication and he returned to work.

Adam noticed that when he handled police calls, he felt hyper-vigilant. Officers always function in an elevated state, but Adam was functioning at an even higher level.

"Every time I'd contact somebody to pat them down, when they'd tense up ..." Adam paused and then continued explaining, "Cops should be aware, but I was paranoid."

About two years had passed since the shooting when Adam was sent to a domestic disturbance call where a woman had been stabbed. The suspect fled and burst into a random house in the neighborhood.

Adam parked a block away and grabbed his rifle before approaching the house. When Adam got there, the front window was shattered and the garage door was open.

"I could see a guy in the living room, holding something," Adam said. "He was looking toward me but not really looking at me. He was looking through me."

Adam was not certain if the man in the house was the suspect or a resident, so Adam called him out.

The man walked up to the shattered window and smashed the remaining glass with a large pair of pruning shears. Then the man went to the kitchen and grabbed a knife.

Rather than entering, Adam and the other police at the scene decided to set a perimeter and contain the house for the SWAT team.

The suspect came into the garage, holding a knife and a pair of pruning shears.

"Drop the weapon," Adam yelled while standing just outside the rollup garage door.

The suspect stood in the center of the garage, growling like a dog, while the officers tried everything to get him to surrender.

"We even shot him in the stomach with a less lethal beanbag shotgun," Adam said. "It didn't faze him whatsoever."

The man looked up at Adam and raised the knife. Then he charged with it extended.

"I don't even remember taking my rifle off safe," Adam said. "I remember the rifle resting on my shoulder, against my cheek, and following him with the red dot from my EOTech sight. I heard the muted sounds of our gunshots, and I saw him falling to the ground.

Then I smelled gunpowder from my rifle. I don't remember squeezing the trigger or how many times I shot."

"It kind of happened in slow motion," Adam said. "Then he was just lying there. I kept saying we were going to help him, but he was already dead. I could see blood puddling from his legs and chest. I thought he was dead, but I wanted the medics coming anyway."

Other officers arrived and handcuffed the suspect before they went to clear the house. Adam started to enter the house until someone stopped him.

"You're not going in the house," Adam's sergeant firmly said when he arrived on scene.

"I'm going to make sure everybody is okay," Adam said.

"No, we have enough bodies," the sergeant said. "You look like you're in control, but I need you to walk away."

In hindsight, Adam thought his sergeant had made the right call. Adam walked down the street and secured his rifle in the sergeant's trunk.

"That's when it clicked," Adam said. "Fuck, I shot this guy."

An officer drove Adam to the station and asked if he was hungry.

"It's the weirdest thing—I realized I was starving," Adam said. "The officer was trying to make me comfortable, so we stopped at In-N-Out Burger."

Adam called his mother to explain that he was ok before she heard the news. Then he called his wife.

"Fuck, again?" she asked. "We're going to go through this again?"

An outside agency came in to do the investigation, and they were very professional. They put Adam and his wife in a hotel room, where he could relax until his interview.

"Are you okay?" Adam's wife asked. "It's okay if you want to cry."

"Honestly, I feel fine," Adam said. "I don't feel anything. I can go to sleep right now."

The investigators took photos of Adam in his uniform and examined his handgun. Once they realized he had not shot his handgun, he was allowed to keep it.

Once Adam's attorney arrived, Adam provided a voluntary statement without any Miranda warning.

"They don't treat you like a suspect," Adam said. "They treat you like a victim. Technically, you are the victim of an attack."

Adam did not experience any anxiety after the shooting, and within a week he was back to work.

Being at work around his friends kept him from sitting at home, dwelling on the shooting, but it did not take long before Adam returned to his careless attitude toward life.

"I went back to drinking, partying, and doing stupid shit I shouldn't have been doing," Adam said. "That's when my career started going downhill. I got blackballed. I was no longer allowed to train people, and I was denied any special assignments."

In hindsight, Adam recognized that he was to blame.

"I was being a dick, dude," Adam said. "When supervisors said something, I would say, 'That's bullshit,' and that type of thing. I was just caustic."

"Then my wife finally called it quits and left me over my shit," Adam said. "At first, I was okay with it, but then I began to realize I hadn't dealt with all my PTSD issues, and that was getting me in trouble."

Adam talked to his psychologist, who decided to give Adam a couple of months away from work to deal with his PTSD. When the police department discovered that Adam was off for stress, he was put on administrative leave and stripped of his badge and gun.

"I had been carrying a gun every day for two months and now I can't?" Adam said. "That pissed me off. What exactly had changed? I hadn't shot anybody or done anything stupid."

Adam felt entitled because of the bad situation the administrators created by trying to save money, which led to the first shooting.

"You motherfuckers owe me," Adam thought. "You guys put me in this position in the first place."

Adam kept working with the psychologist, who suggested a treatment called EMDR, which was recently adopted by the military to treat PTSD.

"At first, I thought it was a bunch of shit," Adam said. "Tapping my hands and moving my eyes are not going to make me feel better."

The psychologist told Adam that PTSD is like a block in your brain, similar to a dam in a river that stops the flow, but if you open the dam, everything runs smooth.

"Okay, I'll try it," Adam told the doctor. "And no shit, dude, within weeks I was feeling better."

Adam said that before the treatment he was pissed off all the time. He likened having PTSD to having a headache every day and then one day waking up without it.

Adam reunited with his wife after a two-year separation.

"We actually get along better now than we ever have," Adam said. "I started feeling a whole lot better, and now I realize what is important. This is just a job, and my family is everything. We worked things out, we live together again, and I couldn't be happier."

Adam was forced to hire a lawyer to get his gun returned and sick time reimbursed. Adam had to jump through some hoops to get back to work by filling in thousands of multiple-choice bubbles on a psych test.

After the psych test, the doctor said, "There's nothing wrong with you. They just panicked. Don't worry about this. You're going back to work tomorrow."

Adam said the most important things he learned from all his experience were to get back to work as soon as possible and resist the temptation to isolate yourself.

"Keep busy with your friends and family," Adam said. "Do something healthy, and avoid drinking."

Adam explained how difficult it is to be in law enforcement, because officers are supposed to be tough and not ask for help.

"If I can prevent somebody from going through what I went through—feeling that loneliness, feeling like I'm going crazy, and then almost losing my family—fuck it," Adam said. "I'll be open with anybody."

BRIAN GLICK

Minutes before Brian Glick's shift ended, police dispatch sent him and his partner to handle a loud party call. When Brian pulled up to the house, several kids wearing dresses and suits were playing in the street.

Brian pulled up directly in front of the house and could hear loud music booming in the backyard. Normally, Brian and his partner would have stopped down the street and walked in, but they were feeling complacent at almost three in the morning. From the driver's seat, Brian called out to a young girl.

"Is this your house?" Brian asked.

"Yes, we're having a quinceañera," the girl answered in broken English.

"Can you get your daddy?"

The girl started walking away, and Brian heard rapid "pop-pop" sounds coming from down the street. Brian looked out the windshield and saw muzzle flashes.

Brian's partner was eating from a bag of Doritos when the shooting started. Chips flew all over the inside of the car when he grabbed the radio to broadcast "Shots fired."

Brian floored the accelerator, and the blacked-out patrol car flew toward a man with a gun. The shooter looked toward the police car and jumped into his Mustang.

"I was 22 years old with only eight months on the job," Brian said. "I was pretty jacked up."

There were few cars on the road at three in the morning, so their pursuit occupied both traffic lanes through the residential neighborhoods.

"He was flying—100 to 110 MPH—all over the city," Brian said. "I could hear other units trying to catch up, but the pursuit kept changing directions."

Brian backed off the accelerator, but the shooter obviously did not know of the upcoming steep drop-off.

"I was already on the brakes and momentarily lost his taillights," Brian said. "When I got to the edge and started heading down the decline, he was already fishtailing out of control."

The Mustang punched through a block wall at 80 MPH, launching cinder blocks and dust everywhere.

"We barely stopped less than a car length behind him," Brian said. "It was way too close for comfort, but as fast as we were going, that was the best I could do."

When the police car skidded to a stop, the other car's driver was already climbing out of the Mustang.

"Jesus, he's alive?" Brian asked. "In that split second, I thought he was going to be dead. Then he was wobbling out of the car, so my mind clicked into a different mode."

The driver ran into the yard, through the broken hole in the wall, and Brian followed.

"You better run, motherfucker," Brian said. "I was jacked up from the pursuit, and I was calling him every name in the book."

Brian's partner climbed on top of the block wall to watch the suspect from a higher vantage point. When the suspect was distracted climbing the fence, Brian hopped into the small yard with the suspect.

"We were about 15 feet away from each other," Brian said. "He was at one end of the yard, and I was at the other."

The suspect finally gave up trying to get over a vine-covered fence. He turned to face Brian and slid down into a squatting position.

Brian was kneeling behind a small lemon tree with a three-inch-thick trunk. It was not cover, but it provided some concealment.

"When the suspect squatted, everything kind of stopped," Brian said. "I remember everything going on; I guess it would be tunnel vision at that point. It all slowed down and I only focused on him."

"Police! Put your hands up!" Brian yelled. "Then the man reached for his waistband and pulled out a gun."

Brian thought "gun," and instantly fired one round. He did not have time to make a conscious decision to shoot; his body took over and reacted when he recognized the weapon. The man instantly fell over to his side and dropped the gun.

"I was carrying a Colt .45," Brian said, "but it sounded like those little white caps you throw on the ground. I remember looking at my weapon to see if it was okay because it sounded like I had a stovepipe or something had gone wrong with my gun."

Brian's partner jumped down from the wall and covered the man while Brian handcuffed him.

"He started mumbling something in Spanish—a prayer or something," Brian said. "We stayed right there on top of him until units got there. It was probably seconds, but it seemed like a long time."

When backup units arrived, Brian felt like he had to help at the scene and write a report.

"I was fresh off of training three months earlier," Brian said. "When you're new, they volunteer you to handle everything, even when it's not your call, so I remember feeling like I had work to do. My training officer was the first guy on scene. He checked that I was ok and threw me in a patrol car."

When Brian got to the station, he went to the locker room to change out of his uniform and waited for homicide investigators. An officer who had been in a shooting approached Brian in the locker room and asked what had happened.

The officer gave Brian a pep talk and encouraged him not to hold back talking about any fear that caused him to shoot the suspect. He also prepared Brian to expect his Miranda rights.

"That calmed me down," Brian said. "They don't go over officer-involved shootings in the academy, so I probably would have gotten shaken up by the Miranda warning had I not known it was coming."

Brian's partner came into the locker room and asked if Brian wanted to pray for the man Brian had shot.

"No, I don't want to pray for him," Brian said. "I don't really care about him right now. I want to pray for me."

Brian was not upset, but at the moment he felt numb and was more concerned about the entire process.

After Brian got dressed, he shut the door to his locker and was startled by his lieutenant.

"He was a tough dude," Brian said. "He was a cowboy and a gun fanatic. He chewed the biggest pinch of dip you can get in your mouth. He sat in the watch commander's office with his feet up on the desk and spit in the trash can all night. We thought he was a kick-ass lieutenant, and all of the young kids looked up to him, including me."

"Hey, Glick," the lieutenant said. "Your dude died. Good job."

Brian started the interview with the homicide investigators, and even though he was prepared, it still felt weird when he was advised of his Miranda rights.

"Their eyes widened when I told them I was 22 and had been working for only eight months," Brian said.

"I knew you were young," one investigator told Brian, "but you really are just a kid. You're gonna be fine. Don't worry about anything."

The interview was straightforward, and when they wrapped up, the investigators warned Brian to avoid the media.

"They're going to make you sound like a killer," one investigator said. "So don't even watch the news."

Brian left the station at about nine that morning with one of his partners, who invited Brian to get a beer. After a couple of drinks, Brian went home and took a nap. When he woke up, the first thing he did was turn on the news. Thankfully, the media had not sensationalized the story.

Brian called his parents. His dad asked if he was ok and offered to come visit. His mother started crying and warned that his job was too dangerous.

"I love my job, Mom," Brian told her. "This is going to happen, but I'm fine. Don't worry about it."

For about a week or two, Brian had digestion problems.

"Everything I ate went right through me," Brian said. "I wasn't depressed. I just wasn't very hungry. I guess your system is a little jacked up. It was really weird."

The department sent Brian to see a psychologist, who asked Brian if he felt that he had done the right thing.

"I told the psych I was satisfied with the decision I had made," Brian said. "I'm not glad I killed someone, but he was a dangerous guy. I feel bad for his family, but to be quite honest, I'd rather his family lose somebody than mine."

There were a couple of times the next year that the shooting crossed his mind when he drove through the neighborhood where it had happened.

"I don't know why, but every time it went through my head, the clearest thing from that night is seeing my partner drop his bag of chips and throw it in the glove box."

The only lasting side effects of the shooting were the frightening dreams.

"It was always a dream where I needed my gun, but it wouldn't work," Brian said. "One time, I dreamt my gun got stuck, like it was cemented in the holster. Another time, I had my finger on the trigger and it would fall to pieces. Another time, the gun melted."

The dreams eventually went away.

CHAD ROBICHAUX

Chad Robichaux's partner frantically called for backup as he raced to a domestic violence call of a man armed with a rifle. When Chad arrived, the man was barricaded in his house and likely on the verge of killing his wife in a domestic violence dispute.

As typically happens in domestic violence calls, the wife turned on Chad and started fighting him when he tried to escort her out of the house. Chad also had to deal with the man with the gun, so out of desperation, he pushed the wife outside and over the porch railing.

Chad's partner went to the window of the room where the man had barricaded himself. Chad went to the front door of the house, near the hallway where the husband was. Chad ordered the suspect to drop his weapon, but the suspect yelled back, demanding that Chad leave his house.

"The rifle was up on his shoulder, with his finger near the trigger," Chad said. "I thought he was taunting me."

Chad continued ordering him to put the gun down.

"Stop or I'm going to kill you," Chad yelled as the man started walking down the hallway, toward him.

"That morning, if you had asked me what I'd do if a guy pointed a gun at me," Chad said, "I would've said, 'Blast him.'"

But it was not that easy, especially once Chad had glanced around the living room full of family pictures and children's toys.

"I felt compassion," Chad said. "It would have been such a permanent decision."

Chad kept his handgun in close and stepped forward. He reached for the barrel of the man's rifle and kicked him in the groin.

"When I grabbed his gun, I really believed I could yank it out of his arms," Chad said. "I still felt like I was in control."

They started fighting over each other's weapons, but the guy was a foot taller and 130 pounds heavier than Chad.

"When he grabbed my hand, I knew I was in trouble, because he was beginning to overwhelm me," Chad said. "I felt composed, but I got pissed. I remember thinking, 'You're going to make me kill you.'"

Chad fired six times. So did his partner.

"We did six-shot rhythm drills at the range," Chad said. "I always wondered if I fired six times because of that training."

Chad vividly remembered his partner shooting over his shoulder, but Chad heard only muffled "pop-pop" sounds.

"My ears never rang at all," Chad said. "But I heard the slide of his gun functioning in slow motion. I always remember how strange that was to me."

The suspect turned and dropped to his knees. He looked back over his shoulder with a surprised look and said, "You killed me."

"I'm sure it happened really fast," Chad said. "But it seemed like he looked back at me in slow motion."

Chad pushed him to the ground and ripped the rifle away. One of the bullets had gone through the suspect's wrist, and he was bleeding everywhere.

"I was fighting his hand to cuff him because all the bones were broken," Chad said. "His hand was like mush in the handcuff."

The man bled all over Chad. With his wife screaming in the background, the man died in front of him.

The man was hit with 11 of the 12 bullets.

"I always joke that my partner was the one who dropped the round," Chad said.

Once the supervisors arrived, things began happening fast.

"I wasn't really worked up," Chad said. "I just remember not believing this just happened. I had a compulsion to go and talk to the wife because she was screaming and freaking out, but they wouldn't let me talk to her."

Chad and his partner were immediately separated and brought to the detective bureau to begin the interviews.

"I wasn't worried I was going to get in trouble or anything," Chad said. "But I was a little apprehensive about giving them my gun."

The detectives explained that seizing the firearm was a normal part of the process, and the chief handed Chad another gun.

Chad went home that night, but no one had notified his wife of what had happened. He woke her and tried to explain what had happened, but she rolled back over and fell back to sleep. This really upset Chad. He struggled all night to sleep because he was still wired.

The next morning, the chief called Chad and warned him not to read the newspapers.

"Of course, I went out and got a newspaper," Chad said. "The front page read 'Cold-Blooded Murder.'"

The newspapers reported that witnesses saw the suspect kneeling, facing away, when the officers shot him in the back. That controversy led the police chief and DA's office to not publicly support the officers.

"I couldn't understand why someone would make statements like that," Chad said. "I thought it was malicious, because the forensic evidence showed that all the bullets entered him from the front."

Chad later realized that the witnesses probably heard the gunshots and then looked to see the suspect kneeling and facing away from the officers.

"The grand jury was extremely scary," Chad said. "I knew there was a potential for indictment for second-degree murder. I remember trying to explain to my wife how serious it was. If the grand jury indicted me, I was going in handcuffs."

There was more than one witness claiming the police had the suspect on his knees, turned away, and that they executed him, but after a weeklong trial, the forensic evidence cleared the officers.

It was not until after the trial that the department publicly supported Chad and his partner. They received the Medal of Valor from the state, and both were promoted to detective.

The department sent Chad to a psychologist, which he thought was a waste of time.

"It was just about clearing me to put me back on duty," Chad said. "I don't really think I was ok after that. I just made do."

One of the most significant consequences of the shooting was a breakdown in his marriage.

"I was really mad at my wife and resented her for years after it," Chad said. "We probably could have used some counseling, but I didn't talk to anybody about it."

When he woke her up the night of the shooting, he misunderstood her lack of response.

"I thought she didn't care," Chad said. "She's always been a bit naïve, which is probably a blessing because of the work I did, but when I went to talk to her about something serious, she just blew me off."

Years later, Chad realized he had come to the wrong conclusion. When he assumed she did not care, she actually just did not understand the significance of the event. That led him to push her away, which later led to their separation.

"The chief thought it was important to get back on the horse," Chad said. "They took us to the range, and I remember the smell of gunpowder overwhelmed me after firing that first round."

After Chad returned to work, he experienced some contradictory emotions about the shooting.

"I felt bad that I felt good about it," Chad said. "But I was also mad at the guy for making me do it."

One of Chad's partners, a former Marine, congratulated him on the shooting and said, "I've been doing this a long time, and I've never gotten to shoot anybody. I can't believe you beat me to it."

The shooting gave Chad a lot of credibility among his peers.

"When people started giving me accolades, it kind of got to my head," Chad said. "I performed well under the ultimate test, and I was highly awarded for it. I felt a bit of bravado and became more aggressive, but then another side of me felt some conviction for not feeling bad."

After the grand jury trial, Chad became jaded toward law enforcement.

"I was pretty bitter afterward," Chad said. "I had a bad attitude, because when it came down to it, they wouldn't have your back."

A couple of years later, when the terrorist attacks of September 11 happened, Chad was already a former active-duty Force Recon Marine and in a Force Recon Reserve unit, so he quickly volunteered to go active duty. Later, he was accepted in the elite Joint Special Operations Task Force and deployed to Afghanistan on and off until 2007, doing special operations with some of the most elite military units fighting the War on Terror.

It was not until after returning to Afghanistan eight more times that Chad began experiencing symptoms of PTSD.

Chad had already been having dreams about interacting with the man he shot, but the anxiety from the pressure of the war became overwhelming.

"I wasn't telling anyone," Chad said. "I just tried to push through it, and I ended up pushing until the wheels flew off."

The stress became so intense that Chad does not remember the last two weeks of his deployment.

"I was having these severe panic attacks," Chad said. "My body would go numb, and my throat felt like it was swelling shut. My body was in a constant state of fight or flight. I just finally broke, and the physiological effects that come with that just continued on."

When he got back to the U.S., he was diagnosed with severe PTSD. "I was pulled from my job, and my wife and I were left to deal with it," Chad said.

One moment Chad was excelling on the task force, and the next moment he was stripped from doing the most amazing job in the world.

"I had quit my law enforcement career," Chad said. "So what was I going to do now?"

At that time, Chad blamed everyone else for his problems. He blamed his father and the military, as well as his wife, because she did not understand what he had been through.

"During that time, I really had a chance to reflect, and I came to the conclusion that it was me," Chad said. "That brought me to a point of deep depression. That was a really low point for me because I would sit in my closet with a pistol."

As a cop, Chad had been on suicide scenes, so he started thinking about who was going to find him and clean up the mess. He was torn with the statistic that one out of three children end up committing suicide following a parent's suicide, and he realized how much his boys already emulated him.

When the divorce papers were ready to be signed, Chad's wife went to his apartment and asked how he could have been so successful in his career, but when it came to his family, he had quit.

"That question ... It really challenged me," Chad said. "She'd asked it many times before, but at that moment ... You know."

Chad said there is a common misconception that many military warriors suffer from PTSD or anxiety because they killed people.

"I don't think any veteran cares about killing Taliban," Chad said. "The real war fighters I come across don't sit awake seeing the faces of Taliban they killed. That's just not reality. Their biggest thing is that they were important and now they're not."

"It's a lack of purpose," Chad said. "For me, the restoration of my faith was really re-finding my purpose."

After leaving the military, Chad found a new purpose when he founded The Mighty Oaks Warrior Foundation, which is a faith-based nonprofit that helps military and first responders recover from the most challenging cases of PTSD.

"I've been to all the counselors, I've been medicated, and I have done all those things, and nothing worked," Chad said. "When I simply made decisions to align my life with being the man I believe God created me to be, this PTSD thing, this anxiety, anger, all these things ... They went away."

DEAN SPIVACKE

Dean Spivacke had just cleared the evening briefing when he received the call of a man threatening to kill himself.

The department had updated to mobile data computers, but they did not buy enough radio repeaters, which left dead spots throughout their rural jurisdiction. Dean missed parts of the radio transmission because the radio kept cutting out.

Dean arrived at the single-story corner house before his canine handler backup arrived. He had parked a house away and started walking when he noticed several kids playing outside. A man was standing in front of the house and another was leaning against a car in the driveway. Dean did not hear a physical description of the suicidal subject, so Dean thought it might be the guy in the driveway.

"Hey, dude. Let me talk to you for a minute," Dean said to the man.

The first man turned and ran for the house while the guy leaning against the car stood there.

"'Well, that's gotta be him,' I thought," Dean said. "I still remember like it was yesterday. He was wearing light brown work boots, white socks pushed down, and those ugly-ass, light blue, Ocean Pacific corduroy shorts."

The front yard of the house was surrounded by an odd chain-link fence that was smashed down and stood only about one foot off the ground. Dean had taken one step over the fence when he noticed all of the windows in the house were smashed out.

"My natural inclination was to chase the guy," Dean said. "But when I noticed the windows, I paused and saw him going through the house."

Dean momentarily lost sight of the man, and seconds later he came running back out the front door.

"I didn't even have time to get my foot back across the fence," Dean said. "He came hauling ass out the front door and made a beeline toward me, with a big-ass, three-foot machete."

Dean was standing about 30 feet away from the front door when he first saw the man return.

"He was running straight at me," Dean said. "I remember him hitting the door, and he got to within 15 or 20 feet away, tops. It scared the shit out of me because he was almost on top of me when I drew my gun."

Dean did not have time to say anything to the man, but in those milliseconds he remembered there were kids standing behind him.

"I remember thinking he couldn't get past me with that machete, because I didn't want him to get to those kids," Dean said.

Dean drew his Glock .45 out of the holster, but he did not make a conscious decision to pull the trigger.

"I just remember sticking the gun out and pulling the trigger," Dean said. "I have no idea how many rounds I fired. I just kept firing until he stopped coming at me."

The investigation later revealed that he had fired nine times.

"I'm not a big shooting kind of guy, and I'm no great shot," Dean said. "But on that day, like a Wyatt Earp who doesn't practice a lot, I was, like, dead on."

After seven of those bullets hit the man, he dropped and landed face first a couple of feet in front of Dean.

"I was watching him go down as the machete came out of his hand, and it slid across the ground and hit me in the foot," Dean said.

Dean keyed his radio microphone to call for an ambulance and heard "bloop-bloop," which meant his radio was not connecting to the repeater.

"To be honest, my radio system caused me more stress than the shooting," Dean said. "I remember getting jacked up because I couldn't tell anybody this had happened, and I needed to get this guy help."

Dean turned around to head for his car, which had a more powerful radio. When he turned around, a car came flying into the driveway. The man's girlfriend jumped out of the car and started screaming. She started running toward her boyfriend, who was on the ground, but Dean stood between them.

"I had my gun in one hand and was fighting her with the other," Dean said. "I was holding on to her for dear life while she was going batshit crazy and screaming like a fucking wombat."

Dean dragged her back to his patrol car.

"I just stuffed her in the back of the car to get her off of me," Dean said. "While she was screaming in the background, I grabbed my unit radio and was able to get out 'Shots fired, deputy involved.'"

When Dean announced the shooting on the radio, a deputy in a different area drove by a man with a gun. The man waved at the deputy and then shot himself in the head.

While Dean was trying to get paramedics and backup, the other deputy announced on the radio that a man had just blown his own head off. Dean's radio kept cutting in and out while a third deputy announced that he was out on an unrelated call of a dead body.

The coincidence of three simultaneous dead bodies overwhelmed the dispatcher. It took a while before she realized they were not the same call. Once the radio traffic was sorted out, Dean got out of the patrol car and began walking back to the man he had shot. Dean never had a chance to handcuff or begin CPR on him.

As he was walking back, a crowd of people began to form. Dean pointed at them and ordered them to back up.

"They turned and ran across the street," Dean said. "I still remember thinking, 'Damn, they sure did listen.'"

Multiple witnesses later said Dean still had his gun in his hand—and pointed it at the citizens—when he ordered them to leave.

"I swear to God, man, I have absolutely no recollection of that," Dean said. "My recollection to this day is that I pointed my finger at them."

When paramedics arrived, they started scooping up the man to transport him to the hospital, but Dean began arguing with them.

"He's dead," Dean said. "Why are you taking him?"

Once backup officers arrived and took over the scene, Dean walked back to his car and broke down crying.

"I could finally turn it off," Dean said. "I didn't have to do anything anymore. It was a complete emotional release."

Dean explained that he had to cope with an overwhelming amount of stress in a couple of minutes. It started with the machete attack; then the man died at his feet, and he fought with the woman. The frustration with the radio was the final straw.

"I wasn't lying on the ground, crying like a baby, but I remember breaking down for a minute," Dean said. "I was embarrassed by that. I was thinking, 'What is wrong with you? You're a cop. Cops don't cry. You don't do that.'"

After a minute in the car, Dean felt as though he had released a giant ball of tension. He got out of the car and got back to business.

He was taken back to the station, where he was interviewed and eventually met with the psychologist. She warned him of several adverse reactions he should expect in the coming weeks, including sleepless nights, sexual dysfunction, and digestive problems.

"What did I get myself into?" Dean wondered after hearing a laundry list of horrible things that were going to happen to him.

About a week later, Dean called the psychologist.

"I need to come in and talk to you," Dean told her. "I'm freaking out over here."

After a week had passed, Dean felt none of the symptoms she had warned him about.

"I had no guilt, no remorse, no feeling about it at all," Dean said. "I was completely apathetic. I didn't give a rat's ass about killing this guy, and that scared me. I worried that I was a cold-blooded killer."

"It's black-and-white in your mind," the psychologist explained. "There's no doubt in your mind that what you did was right. There's not even a slight hint of question. He came at you with a machete, and you defended yourself—end of discussion."

Dean described the dreams that almost every young police officer experiences—the dreams where you cannot pull the trigger, or the bullet falls out of the gun.

"The weirdest thing," Dean said, "was that after the shooting, in every one of those dreams, the gun always worked, and I won every single time."

Dean went to a follow-up psychologist interview with his canine handler partner and their wives. The doctor went around the room and asked each of them how he or she was doing.

"I'm fine," Dean said. "Everything's golden."

His wife and the canine handler partner said the same thing, but Dean's partner's wife had a different story.

"He's being an asshole," the canine handler partner's wife said. "He's not eating right. He's treating me terribly, and he's yelling at the kids."

Dean explained that his partner had had a completely different reaction to the shooting. The partner thought he was doing ok, but he was not. The stress of the shooting triggered medical problems, and four weeks later he had a severe asthma attack and died.

Dean did not walk away from the shooting without at least a hint of post-traumatic stress. In the months following the shooting, he felt anxiety every time he tried to use his radio.

"Every time I put out traffic stops or a pedestrian check, my blood pressure would go through the roof," Dean said. "I stopped using the radio, because every time it didn't work, I'd get pissed off and take it out on the dispatcher."

After a month of arrests with no radio traffic, Dean's sergeant called Dean in and lectured him.

Five months later, Dean was sent to a domestic violence call of a man threatening his wife with a gun. Dean pulled up to the rural mobile home that sat on top of a hill.

"There was no way for me to get to the house without being exposed," Dean said.

When Dean got there, he grabbed his rifle and walked around toward the back of the house. Dean could not see the house clearly, so he had to move across an open yard.

"The husband popped out the door and started firing at me," Dean said. "I saw the muzzle flash, and I felt the impact of the bullets hitting me. He was shooting the shit out of me."

Dean started returning fire and kept running until he got behind a shed.

"I thought I was dead, because he hit me several times," Dean said. "I felt nothing. I couldn't feel any pain or blood—nothing. I'm thinking, 'This is what it's like to die. I can't feel anything.'"

Dean stood behind the shed and peeked around the corner. Dean was angry. He wanted to go after the man.

"I was mad as hell that he had killed me, and I wanted to kill that motherfucker," Dean said.

Dean explained that he felt anxious when he first got on scene because he knew the man had a gun, but once the man started shooting, he was no longer afraid.

"I'm not fearless by any stretch of the imagination," Dean said. "It just happened too quickly for me to be scared. It didn't even occur to me to be afraid."

Seconds passed and the front door slammed open. The man stepped out on the porch and yelled, "You shot me."

"I brought the rifle up," Dean said. "Oh, yes, I wanted to shoot him. I thought I was dead, but I felt aggressive. I wanted to catch this guy."

Dean was peeking around the corner of the shed when he watched the man topple over and land on the raised porch. Dean and another deputy slowly approached the man. After they handcuffed the man, Dean took inventory of his own body.

"Everything was still working," Dean said. He had looked down and seen no blood, but he noticed he was covered in dirt. "Where did all this dirt come from?" he had wondered.

Dean could not figure out how he was still alive, because he was certain he had been shot multiple times. Dean went back to where he had been when the man had opened fired. The ground a few feet in front of where he was standing was covered in little divots.

"He was dropping the rounds on the ground in front of me," Dean said. "He was shooting low. It was gravel that was popping up and hitting me in the face and chest."

If the man had been a better shot, Dean would have been killed.

"I did not make a conscious decision to shoot at all," Dean said.

"It was the same thing as with the first guy. It didn't occur to me that he was going to come out of the house with a machete. I didn't even think about that."

Six months later, Dean and another deputy were in a car pursuit of a stolen car with a wanted parolee. During the car chase on a dark rural road, the parolee and his girlfriend kept aiming a bright spotlight out of the back of the car to blind the officers

"It was literally a million candlepower spotlight," Dean said. "It was about 10 times brighter than a police spotlight."

As the pursuit continued, the suspect missed a 90-degree turn and crashed into a hillside. After the crash, the spotlight came back on, and then the parolee started shooting at the deputies.

"We shot the shit out of that car," Dean said. "We did, like, $40,000 worth of damage to the car."

The suspect and the girlfriend buried themselves under the dashboard as the bullets flew through the car and right over their heads.

Moments later, the girlfriend came running out of the car, and Dean and his partner took her into custody. Seconds later, the parolee threw the gun out and surrendered.

After everything settled down, detectives came out for the investigation. One of the detectives walked up to Dean and said, "There's no way you're the shooter."

"It was me," Dean said.

"You've got to be kidding me," the detective said. "Again?"

After the second and third shootings, Dean did not have any type of an emotional breakdown like he had following the first shooting.

"Guys go their entire career and don't get in one shooting," Dean said. "I didn't want to tell anybody, but shortly afterward, I thought it was pretty cool that I had been in three shootings in 12 months."

Following the third shooting, Dean felt more confident on the job. All of Dean's career experience—including working homicide, working as a dog handler, working in SWAT, and teaching at the academy—all boosted his conviction.

"I felt a little bit like Superman," Dean said. "I got that tombstone courage, which was stupid, but I felt that if it happened again, I could deal with it."

"As a lieutenant, I suck," Dean said. "I'm a shitty administrator, but if the world's falling apart, I'm the guy you want next to you. I'm no superhero, but for whatever reason, God has graced me with that ability, and I appreciate that in this career."

The department expressed no concern after all three shootings.

"It was still a little bit of old school," Dean said. "Now everybody gets mollycoddled and they want someone to hold their hand. Back then, they're like, 'Is there a bone sticking out? Rub some dirt in it and get back to work.'"

Dean said he never experienced any long-term trauma after the shootings.

"I really just didn't give a damn," Dean said. "I knew there was a chance that it could happen. I survived and I got some awesome stories to tell, so let's move on."

But Dean said his wife might have a different perspective. They have been married for many years and have a strong relationship.

"I suspect there might be some times when she's seen some stuff that I haven't, because obviously I have my perception, but we've never had issues," Dean said. "Perhaps that's your follow-up book—*Spouses of Officers Who've Been in Shootings*—because you will probably get more emotion out of them."

Dean never called his wife from work because he was always too busy, but Dean called her after both of the first two shootings. When he called her after the third, she answered the phone by asking, "You got in another shooting, didn't you?"

When Dean worked as a homicide detective and later as a homicide supervisor, he investigated about 500 homicides and roughly 150 officer-involved shootings. Dean has a unique perspective on officer-involved shootings from having been in and investigating them.

"I've seen guys that fired and missed one round and had to retire because they couldn't believe they had to shoot their gun," Dean said. "You don't have to practice at the range a thousand times, but you have to have in your head that this could happen."

Dean's experience was that officers who struggled emotionally after their shootings were usually not mentally prepared to be in a shooting.

"You can't walk around with your head in the sand, thinking it's never going to happen," Dean said. "Practicing officer safety is important, but it still doesn't replace your mental preparedness and thinking that this could happen."

Dean explained that many of the officers that had emotional struggles afterward often handled the situation appropriately, but they could not handle the aftermath.

"I think I should probably care more than I do, but I really don't," Dean said. "It's not my fault. If you do your thing and have to get shot, that's not my choice. I'm coming home at the end of the day."

"We so badly want it to be a kinder, gentler place," Dean said. "Everybody's so afraid of litigation, so they're afraid to talk about an officer killing somebody. Everyone wants to close their eyes and push it away. Everybody wants to be an administrator and worry about the wrong things instead of worrying that bad stuff happens in the world. There are fucked-up people walking around this world, and it's our job to deal with them. It's not our job to deal with this other nonsense. People keep losing sight of that, and it drives me crazy."

GREG CARROLL

Greg Carroll was driving down a dark side street when he passed a car matching a murder suspect's vehicle description.

Moments earlier, the police dispatcher had reported a shooting in a 7-11 parking lot.

"Holy fuck," Greg thought when he looked back and caught three letters of the license plate. "That's the car."

A shot of adrenaline surged through Greg, but he made an effort to stay calm on the radio.

"I've got the vehicle," he told dispatch.

Greg whipped around and pulled in behind the car. It made a quick left turn and immediately pulled over on a dark residential street.

Greg lit his spotlight just as the driver jumped out of the car, with a cocked pistol in his right hand.

Two other passengers got out of the car and started flanking Greg to his right.

"I'm all alone, and this was going fast," Greg said. "There was so much going on, but it's amazing all the little stuff I remember."

When Greg jumped out of the police car, his radio microphone fell from his shirt and out of reach.

Greg stood in the open doorway of his patrol car and pointed his pistol at the man with the gun, just like he had drilled in training.

"Bájale la pistola," Greg yelled in his rudimentary Spanish.

Instead of putting the gun down, the man stretched his arms down and to the side as he puffed up his chest, taunting Greg.

Greg yelled for the passengers to stop, but they ignored him and moved toward a large tree.

"Holy shit," Greg thought. "These guys are going to come up and ambush me."

Greg, fumbling to find his radio microphone, kept yelling for the driver to drop the gun.

"Send me Code Three backup," Greg said when he had found it.

Greg realized that the passengers did not have weapons in their hands, but he kept getting distracted, looking back and forth between the driver and passengers.

"God damn it," Greg lectured himself. "Get back on the guy with the gun."

When Greg looked back at the driver, he saw a car was driving up toward him.

The car abruptly stopped next to the man with a gun.

"The first thing that came to mind was that some dumb fucking citizen was rolling up on this thing to get in the middle of another police shooting," Greg explained.

His police department had experienced two controversial shootings, and officers were receiving a lot of vocal criticism and public interference.

Greg could not see the car that pulled up because it was concealed behind its headlights. As soon as the car stopped, the driver's door opened and the man with the gun started raising his arm toward the driver, only four feet away.

"There was a lot going on in my mind," Greg said. "I was thinking to myself, 'I'm going to have to shoot this fucker.'"

The man had been holding the gun aimed downward, but now he raised the gun.

Greg lined up his sights on the man's chest, closed one eye, and pulled the trigger.

"They train us to keep firing until the guy goes down, but as soon as I fired, he just dropped like a ton of bricks," Greg said. "They say it never happens like in the movies, but it was just like a movie."

Greg heard a "pop-pop" sound, so he thought he had fired two rounds.

The investigation later revealed that Greg shot only once and hit the man in the chest.

The autopsy showed that "his heart had just exploded," Greg said. "It was almost gone. That's what dropped him so fast."

After the man had gone down, Greg saw his lieutenant step out of the car door that had opened a second earlier. At that moment, Greg realized the car that had driven up was an unmarked police car.

In hindsight, Greg wished he had told the dispatcher the direction of his traffic stop, but it all happened in seconds. There was no time.

"I remember looking back and realizing the whole thing lasted less than a minute," Greg said. "That was fast, because it seemed like a long time."

After the driver had gone down, Greg focused on the two passengers. Greg had been worrying about them the entire time, but this time when Greg pointed his gun at them, they immediately surrendered and went to the ground.

Greg walked up to the man he had shot as several police cars started arriving with their lights and sirens blaring.

"When I took the gun away to cuff him, I distinctly remember that it was cocked," Greg said. "It makes sense, because he had just shot the guy at 7-11."

This detail is where Greg questioned his own memory.

When the driver first got out of the car, Greg clearly remembered seeing that the gun was cocked. Today, he questions if he later added this detail to his memory after seeing the hammer cocked when cuffing the shooter.

Greg had been on the scene of plenty of officer-involved shootings, so he knew his role was to step out of the investigation.

"I just shot this guy," Greg thought as he stood at the scene, taking it all in. "It was kind of surreal."

The sergeant arrived on scene and started accounting for the bullets.

Greg had not realized that in those split seconds, the lieutenant managed to get his weapon out of the holster and fired twice. Both of those bullets missed and hit a nearby building.

The investigation revealed that Greg had fired only one round, and he believes the "pop-pop" sound he heard was from the lieutenant's gun, not his own.

Detectives brought Greg and the lieutenant to an office with two other officers, presumably to witness that they did not compare notes.

Greg understood the process and was confident he had made the right decision, but he picked up the phone and called an attorney. Greg was the police union president and had the attorney on speed dial.

The attorney reminded Greg not to talk about the shooting, and they scheduled to meet at the station in the morning.

While Greg and the attorney were at the office, the off-duty police chief showed up with pizzas and told war stories to keep the mood light.

Greg stepped outside for some air and was replaying everything in his mind.

The chief met Greg outside.

"Are you okay?" the chief asked.

"Yeah, I'm fine," Greg said.

"Don't worry about anything," the chief said. "We're behind you."

That support was comforting. It was one less thing he had to worry about.

Greg later learned the chief's philosophy on shootings was always to support the officer. No cop ever wants to be in a shooting, and 99% of the time the cop makes the right decision.

Greg eventually made it home at about three or four in the morning. His wife was awake and already knew what had happened. She knew not to ask too much.

"I didn't sleep well," Greg said, "probably because of adrenaline and all that, but I managed to get two hours of sleep."

At 8:30 that morning, Greg was back at the station with his attorney to provide a voluntary statement to the investigators.

After a couple of hours of sleep, Greg managed to get through the two-hour interview in a groggy fog.

Greg remembered his attorney debating with the investigators about Miranda rights. The attorney did not want the rights to be read because Greg was providing a voluntary statement.

"It was a little weird sitting there while they read stuff I'm used to reading to somebody else," Greg said.

Then there was debate about having Greg provide a blood sample to investigators.

"I remember them going back and forth," Greg said, "but I didn't care."

The investigators treated Greg very well, so he felt bad when his attorney forced them to write a search warrant for his blood sample.

During the interview, Greg was able to remember the entire shooting as well as he can today. After the interview, Greg went to his mother's house with his wife.

"She offered to make lunch, probably just to make sure I wasn't all stupid or something," Greg said as stoically as he told the rest of the story.

"I was getting really tired," Greg said. "I don't think I could have gone to sleep, because you start replaying it all in your mind."

Greg's wife invited him to step outside. She had been a cop for almost as long as he had, so she knew just when to ask what had happened.

"I unloaded on her," Greg said. "I got to go through everything. I could talk freely. It was just what I needed."

Greg went home and slept well. It wasn't until later that the dreams began. He was given about a month of administrative leave while detectives completed the shooting investigation. Greg took that time to relax at a lake. After that month, Greg had a recurring dream of a man in his bedroom.

"You know when you are in a dream, but you're telling yourself you're awake?" Greg stated. "I remember waking up in the night and panicking. I never saw the guy's face, but I always knew it was him. What's he doing in my room? Why's he standing next to me?"

"Fuck, that was real," Greg would think after waking up. "Wouldn't that be great if I grabbed my gun and started shooting my computer in the middle of the night?"

Greg used to keep a gun in his nightstand, but he moved it because of the dreams.

With time, the dreams faded away, but years later they would resurface when he experienced political stress while serving as the president of the police union.

As the stress increased, the dreams returned, but these dreams were a little different. In these dreams, his bullets would tumble out of his gun in slow motion and hit the suspect, with no effect.

Greg did not understand what had triggered the dreams. He was convinced there was nothing else he could have done during the shooting, and the more Greg contemplated it, the more he realized he should have actually shot the man sooner because of how close he was to the lieutenant when raising the gun.

Greg wanted to talk to a professional to see if there was something that might be causing the dreams. He found an out-of-town therapist that specialized in police officers. They talked for about 45 minutes.

"Everything you've described is normal," the therapist said. "Things should get better over time. Don't worry about it."

That was comforting and helped Greg understand that he was not experiencing anything unusual. The dreams stopped shortly thereafter.

"The department never asked if I wanted to go talk to somebody," Greg said.

He went to the police chief and suggested that it be mandatory that officers see a therapist after a shooting. The chief was old school and asked why.

"Because if somebody needs help, they're not going to ask," Greg answered. "It gives them an out if they are having issues and need to go."

Many years later, Greg avoided driving down the street where the shooting occurred.

"Every time I was in that area, I thought about the shooting," Greg said. "I wasn't shaking or scared, but why go there?"

JOHN DAVIS

At about three in the morning, John Davis drove toward a disturbance complaint of a man racing the engine of his parked car. After John turned a corner, he was forced to park at an angle facing the parked car.

"It wasn't a great tactical spot to be in," John said, "but I was the second car on scene, so it kind of left me no other option."

John aimed his spotlight on the parked car's windshield and gazed at the man seated in the driver's seat.

"I can still see him clearly in my mind," John said. "I can see his face—the thick, dark mustache and brown hair. He was definitely under the influence of something—probably speed. He stuck his head out the window and was moving around erratically. He looked oblivious to what was going on."

John stepped out of his patrol car.

"It all happened really quickly," John said. "You get that sixth sense, so I pulled my gun out as I shut my door."

The man floored the accelerator and steered the car toward John.

"My weapon came up and I was firing while retreating backward," John said. "It felt like that car was right on top of me."

John said there was no time to make a conscious decision to draw his weapon and shoot.

"Delay will usually get you killed," John said. "The decision comes from your training and mindset. I never had to shoot anyone in the military, but I was in several combat situations. My mindset was to always be prepared for the worst—because I'm going home at night."

Somehow John was able to duck behind the bumper of his car a split second before the car raced past him.

The car was riddled with bullets, but none hit the driver. The suspect sped away, and John jumped in his car to chase him. By the time John caught up, the suspect had crashed his car and hopped a fence into a backyard. When John got over the fence, the suspect was running through the yard.

"He made a movement and reached for his waistband," John said. "I gave commands: 'Let me see your hands.'"

John thought the man was either reaching for a weapon or trying to commit suicide.

"I thought I was going to shoot him in the backyard," John said. "If he would have turned around with his hand on his waistband, I would have shot him. I could have easily justified it, but I didn't feel like I had to. He showed me his hands and proned out."

John did not feel fear or anger while in the backyard.

"This guy just tried to kill me, but I felt calm and in control," John said. "I was just reacting to what was going on, but there was no doubt that I was going to catch this guy."

John reflected on his feelings that followed his first shooting.

"The ultimate test for a man is how we react in combat or

life-threatening situations," John said. "I like to test myself. I think I handled it well and remained in control."

Many years later, John was assigned to work day watch in the East End, away from the ghettoes he normally worked during his graveyard shifts. On day watch, the department focus was on verbal judo and community-oriented policing.

"It was ridiculous," John said. "I don't write tickets and do that stuff. I beat up gangsters and put bad people in jail. I'm a cop."

While on day watch, John was sent to a domestic violence call on a lesbian couple. While John was talking to the victim, her girlfriend, in a car, came ripping around the corner and abruptly stopped in the driveway. The driver started screaming at her girlfriend and then sped away.

After clearing the call, John researched the driver and found that she was a third-strike gang member wanted for a parole violation because of her connection with a robbery and shooting.

"They wanted community policing," John said, "so I made her my COPPS project and went hunting for her."

Weeks later, John found her near her car. John jumped out of his patrol car, and she immediately reached for her waistband. John had been warned that she always carried a butterfly knife, so he assumed she was reaching for one.

"I saw something shiny," John said. "I drew down on her and started giving her commands."

The woman continued fumbling with the object at her waistband while John speculated that she was trying to open a butterfly knife. After a few seconds, she got frustrated, jumped in her car, and sped off.

John chased her in a wild car pursuit. She crashed into multiple cars, slid out, made a U-turn, and began racing toward his patrol car.

"I was stuck in a horrible position," John said. "She whipped around and started flying right toward me. I thought she was going to ram me."

Instead of crashing into John's patrol car, she slowed down on a narrow residential street, and drove alongside his car and started shooting.

"She was wacked out of her mind on meth," John said. "I can still see her crazy face, and the gun going back and forth as she's shooting, but the weird thing is, I didn't hear it."

John flipped his car around and continued chasing her until she crashed and rolled her car. For the first time during the incident, John felt nervous when he pulled up to the crash scene and lost sight of her.

"I jumped out of the car, and she was gone," John said. "I didn't see her get out."

John felt in control again when he saw her running up ahead. John caught up to her at the end of a driveway, and she turned and raised her gun to him.

"There was a slight pause at that point," John said. "It's kind of an epic moment. She turned around and I saw the gun. The gun started coming up, so I started firing. I distinctly remember her body absorbing the impact of the bullets and making her body move around like a dance."

When the woman collapsed to the ground, officers started doing first aid. John stood over her, processing what had just happened. She had 19 entry and exit wounds, but surprisingly she was still alive.

"It was weird. I wasn't fired up, but all the other officers were," John said. "I looked down at her and asked, 'Josie, why did you do that?'"

"Why did you fucking kill me?" the woman screamed in a raspy, pain-ridden voice.

When the paramedics began treating Josie, John noticed that one of the bullets had fallen out of her and hit the ground.

"I thought, 'I just fired that,'" John said. "It was surreal."

In the weeks following that shooting, the accumulation of trauma from a career in law enforcement began to surface.

"We literally see the worst parts of our society every day," John said, "and you just push them away."

John investigated a case where an 11-year-old was sodomized multiple times by her uncle.

"I was enraged," John said. "I wanted to find him and kill this dude."

John never pursued the man, but in that moment, John was deeply affected by the pain the rapist caused the child. When John coached his son's football team, he would look at the parents and contemplate the darkness he saw as a police officer and the violence he was forced to inflict when arresting criminals.

"If these people knew what I did last night, would they let me coach their kids?" John asked. "That's why you lose connection with civilians. They can't understand, so you start disconnecting."

John was disconnecting not only with the public but also at home.

"I had no relationship with my wife," John said. "As a cop, these things are not supposed to bother us, so I had no one to express it to."

That second shooting triggered a conscious shift in John's thinking.

"I've been saved too many times," John said. "I'm going to die on this job, so I want to start enjoying life."

About two weeks after that shooting, John was approached by the girl he had had a crush on as a teenager. They started having an affair for a while, and then he started seeing other women too.

"I remember another police officer asked me once if I would I ever cheat on my wife," John said. "I said I would never, ever even think about it, and I meant it 100%. Then, five years later, my heart was corrupted."

Eventually, guilt caught up with John, and he left his wife.

Things continued until one day he was in the sergeant's office being written up. Two weeks prior, John had responded to an officer's emergency plea for help on the radio. John was nearby when the deputy screamed for help, but the deputy was in a bordering city, forcing John to leave his assigned area.

"Are you serious?" John asked the administrator, who was known for petty discipline. "I'm going to go handle this call of a man with a gun, and I'll come back and sign this later."

John raced to the call, where a man was barricaded in his house, writing a suicide letter explaining why he was planning to kill several people on a list. When John arrived on scene, a family member explained that the suicidal man was on the living room couch, with a gun in his waistband.

Eventually, the on-scene sergeant picked his three most-trusted cops to go into the house to confront the man.

"We went in there and had him at gunpoint, demanding to see his hands," John said. "The guy looked up, dropped his pen, reached into his waistband, and started coming up with the gun."

All three officers shot multiple times. When the dust settled, they walked outside, and John noticed one of his partners was smiling.

"What the heck?" John said. "There are people around. Don't be smiling."

John explained that he did not want to give the appearance that they were celebrating killing somebody.

"That's not what my partner was doing at all," John said. "He had been a great cop for a long time, but that was his first shooting. It was really just nervousness."

While John witnessed his partners' reactions after the shooting, John felt nothing.

"I knew what I did was right and justified," John said, "but I wondered why this stuff doesn't bother me."

After this shooting, John went to a psychologist.

"I wasn't that cop who grew up with a silver spoon," John said. "I grew up down there with the people I was working with. I've been in combat and seen death and the carnage of life, so I didn't think this stuff was going to affect me. We act like it doesn't affect us, but looking back now, I can see it definitely started changing me. It was a slow progression."

"After 10 years as a police officer, all the things I saw, and the person I became ..." John said. "It wasn't a person I was proud of."

There were times when John would sit holding a gun, look at it, and wonder.

"Life sucks right now," John said. "Probably the only thing that really prevented me from planning and acting on it was my kids. I would never do that to them."

"I wasn't suicidal, but I didn't care either," John said. "I was doing stupid things like walking in alleys at night by myself, looking for gangs."

John became addicted to the adrenaline rush of violent conflict.

"Those times of violence ... those times when my life was on the line were honestly the only times I had peace," John said. "If I met some gangster in an alley and got into a crazy fight, nothing else was going on at that moment ... just the feeling of control, and not feeling anything other than being in the zone, focused on what's going on. You're not thinking about feelings. You're just reacting. You're in the moment."

John never turned to drugs or alcohol to cope. Instead, he turned to women and the adrenaline rush that comes with being an aggressive police officer.

"I never did anything unethical as a cop," John said, "but I took something that was noble and I made it something very corrupt because of what was going on inside me."

John spent about a year working with the psychologist.

"My psychologist was really smart because he didn't push too hard," John said. "He was like a friend who asked really good questions."

The final straw came when the psychologist brought up the idea of retirement.

"You know, John, you had all these shootings," the psychologist said. "You've been lucky you've had clean shootings, but what if you get into a gray one? I don't want you to end up in jail."

The day of his third shooting was the last day John worked as a police officer.

"I didn't want my life to end up where it was headed," John said. "That was a moment of clarity. I needed to get my life in order."

John medically retired and is able to look back proudly on his career accomplishments. He is grateful for the lessons he learned along the way.

Today, John is able to pass those lessons on through his work at The Mighty Oaks Warrior Foundation, a nonprofit that helps people struggling with PTSD.

"It's really your choice in how you set your life up," John said. "My faith in Christ was strong when I began as a police officer, but without accountability I was living outside of God's plan. If you don't have people to hold you accountable, if you don't have a strong faith, if you don't have your morals set in place, and if you're not open with your wife ... In other words, if you don't have a clear plan for dealing with the trauma of being a police officer, you will fail."

JOHN MILLER

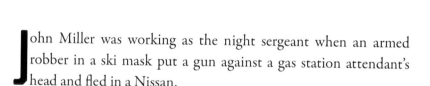

John Miller was working as the night sergeant when an armed robber in a ski mask put a gun against a gas station attendant's head and fled in a Nissan.

"I'm on the highway, behind the champagne-colored Nissan Altima," an officer advised on the radio. "It's occupied by two."

"Don't light him up yet," John replied. "We're coming to you."

When John pulled up behind the suspect's car, he noticed the driver, but there were no passengers. The driver looked at John, shook his head, and floored the accelerator.

The suspect raced through a construction zone on the busy highway and crashed into 12 different cars. John pulled ahead of the Nissan as it was entering a crowded bridge. The suspect rear-ended John, spinning the police SUV 180 degrees.

Pedestrians were everywhere, so the officers were forced to rush the robber's car and order the driver out at gunpoint.

"I grabbed the driver, threw him on the ground, and held him under my knee," John said. "Then the second guy popped up from underneath the glove box."

John kneeled over the driver, only a few feet from the open driver's side door. One officer stood to John's right, and a state trooper stood to his left.

"I had no idea he was firing until I saw the trooper get hit by the bullet," John said. "He hit the officer standing on my right, and then I saw the trooper get hit."

After the trooper went down, John looked through the open door on the driver's side and realized the passenger was holding a gun.

"There was nobody there except for me and him," John said. "He was just five feet away, and I was fixated on him and that gun—tunnel vision. Everything else was blacked out."

John fired three rounds into the car, and the passenger slumped over into the driver's seat.

"I swear to God, I was able to see those bullets leave the barrel of my gun and hit him in the chest," John said. "It was complete silence—slow motion—and when the bullet hit, his shirt ruffled."

During the shooting, John felt like he was in complete control of the situation.

"It just happened so fast that muscle memory took over," John said. "But afterward, I was screaming on the radio, 'Shots fired! Shots fired! I need an ambulance.'"

John was the only supervisor on scene, so he had officers drive the wounded officers to the hospital in police cars. John stood by, trying to protect the crime scene, but people from other agencies started showing up and kicking shell casings all over the place.

John glanced around the crime scene and could not find the gun, money, or ski mask.

"Holy shit," John recalled saying. "Did I shoot the right kid? Was he even part of the robbery?"

After about 20 minutes, John came down from the adrenaline high and realized stress was causing him to second-guess himself.

He did not see the ski mask because it was rolled up on the man's forehead and it looked like a knit cap. The money was balled up in the suspect's pocket, and an officer had already secured the weapon in a patrol car.

The major crimes unit arrived to take over the shooting investigation. They told John to return to the station to collect his uniform and gun.

"I didn't want to go to the PD," John said. "My fatherly instinct was taking over, and I wanted to go see how my guys were."

Even though John understood the process, being the focus of the investigation was still uncomfortable.

"You go from the high of feeling like a hero or something ... to being treated like a criminal," John said. "But I knew the major crimes unit had a job to do."

John walked the investigators through the shooting scene on the bridge.

"I stopped explaining when I got to pulling the trigger," John said. "Because now it was a criminal investigation."

Initially, John blew off the woman from the police department's employee assistance program, but the chief insisted he talk to her before heading home.

"Don't be surprised if you have diarrhea tomorrow," the woman explained. "Your body keeps producing adrenaline for hours afterward and it causes diarrhea."

"I was like, 'You're crazy. I'm out of here,'" John said. "But thank God she told me that."

John went home, and he did not realize until hours later that he had injured his back in the car accident. He went to the hospital that night and needed four weeks to recover. It took the major crimes unit nine months to finish the investigation, but, off the record, they cleared John as soon as he recovered from his back injury.

"I never met with a shrink, but I regret that," John said. "When it first happened, I didn't think anything was wrong. I signed up for this shit—I knew it could happen. So I sucked it up and kept going."

John returned to work and got back into his routine as a patrol sergeant. One night, after picking up a pizza, he pulled up next to another sergeant just as a call came in that was around the corner. A woman reported that her boyfriend was on a crack binge and had stolen her car. The other sergeant went to the call so John could eat dinner in his car.

"All of a sudden, he was screaming on the radio," John said.

"He has a gun and he tried to run me over," the other sergeant yelled into the radio.

John threw the pizza on the floorboard and raced around the corner. The suspect took off, and the two sergeants raced after him. The car pursuit flew through backstreets, until the suspect crashed into a backyard and his car got hung up on a fence.

"He was trying to go forward and reverse to break loose," John said. "I pulled my car behind him so he couldn't get out, and I took cover in the A-frame of my car."

From inside the car, the suspect began taunting the officers with a gun.

"He was pointing it out the back window," John said. "Not quite 180 degrees, but he was waving it about 90 degrees toward us."

The suspect kept waving the gun while the offers repeatedly ordered him to drop it.

"Eventually, he did a 180 and pointed the gun out the back window, right at me," John said. "I let two rounds go and hit him."

The suspect slumped over, but he was still moving, so the officers continued ordering the driver to throw the gun out the window.

A state trooper showed up with a K9, and John asked him to send the dog.

"I'm not sending my dog in there," the trooper said. "He has a gun."

"I was pissed," John recalled of the incident. "That's what the dog is for."

Several officers ended up approaching the car and ripped the suspect through the blown-out rear window. They cuffed him and found a second gun in his waistband.

"By the time we pulled him out of the car and cuffed him, he had already bled out in the car," John said. "That was when my head started going south."

John was standing there when a commander showed up.

"I can't believe it's you again," the commander said.

The commander took a phone call from the chief and said the chief had one question: "What color is the guy?"

The agency was dealing with pressure from the community over another police shooting where officers had killed a black teen at the end of a car pursuit. Prior to that shooting, the illegal immigrant population had made numerous complaints because they were being deported for driving unlicensed.

"Who gives a shit what color he is?" John said. "I didn't come here and pick this; the suspect chose this today."

It made John furious that the chief inquired about the suspect's ethnicity while ignoring that John and his family would have to endure the stress and trauma that followed a police shooting.

John grabbed the dead man by the collar of his shirt and lifted him several inches off the ground.

"You motherfucker," John yelled at the dead body. "I have to tell my wife and my mother that we have to go through this shit again."

After John's first shooting, it took nine months before he was cleared by investigators.

"For nine months, I was in the media," John said. "They go through your personnel file, they question your decision-making, and I lost money sitting at home."

After the second shooting, John was transferred to the detective bureau to keep him off the streets until he was cleared to return to work.

"I wouldn't sit on a desk," John said. "If they had put me on a desk, I would have felt like I did something wrong."

Eventually, John met with a psychologist and was cleared to return to work, but he was still very angry.

"As I reflect back, I realize I was unraveling," John said. "There's no doubt it was the second one that turned me. I was a mess out there. I was drinking a lot, and I wouldn't say no to any overtime. I felt like I had to be there because I didn't want anything to happen to my guys."

The car pursuits caused John's anxiety because he feared calling his family to explain that he had been in another shooting.

"Every time we had a pursuit, I would get all pissed off at the suspect," John said. "They didn't understand the amount of damage that can come from these things."

John's wife also noticed that he had become short-tempered, and she complained that he was at work all the time.

"I had to be at work," John said. "I was waiting for that big one to come to make sure everyone was on their A game. I began to criticize people for not being prepared, and I would harp on the little things."

While John was critical of his officers, he was simultaneously being reckless.

"I stopped wearing a vest and carrying a gun," John explained. "It bothered my back, and I reasoned that it can't happen a third time. I had already been in two, so what were the odds of a third?"

After some time passed, John arrived on a scene after officers arrested a man at the end of a foot pursuit.

"The kid kept running his mouth and talking shit," John said.

As they were putting the suspect in the back of the patrol car, he threatened to find the officers' families.

"I just snapped and jabbed the kid with a slight punch to the chest," John said. "I warned him that if he talked like that at the station, somebody was probably going to put his head through a wall."

"Looking back, I should've retired earlier," John said. "That second shooting affected me. That wasn't me. I had become a different person."

Another officer was uncomfortable with the jab and reported John to a supervisor. The supervisor interviewed the kid, but he was not bothered by it. The kid did not want to make a complaint, so the issue was dropped—until the Department of Justice stepped in.

After ongoing tension in the community, city hall invited DOJ to come in and review the department for racial discrimination.

"It was a political nightmare," John said. "They wanted my chief out, so DOJ came in and tore the place up."

During the DOJ review, investigators learned about the incident when John jabbed the kid in the chest.

"I wasn't going to deny it," John said. "I admitted it happened. It was excessive force, but it never met the level of an indictment."

John had never received a single complaint or been sued for racial discrimination. Both of the men he shot were white, and so was the kid he jabbed, but DOJ was determined to hang someone.

"They wanted my chief out and they wanted to tear my department up," John said. "The feds indicted me for the jab, plus three other officers."

John was offered probation in exchange for a plea agreement.

John never told anyone at the department, but he had begun seeing a psychologist on his own. After numerous discussions, John realized the best thing for himself and his family was to get out of law enforcement.

"I'll never forget the day I filled out my retirement paperwork," John said. "I took a plea deal to put it behind me and move on with my life. It's one of the best things I ever did. You can't know the weight that was off my shoulders to no longer worry about pulling that trigger."

At a hearing, the judge reversed the agreement, and John was sentenced to four months in federal camp.

"It was kind of a joke," John said. "It was basically a small college campus with no fence. The only people that got punished were my wife and kids. I was working out and playing softball every day."

Before John retired, he was serving as the police union president. In retirement, he is employed by the union to represent officers during contract negotiations and discipline, and he also gives lectures on the aftermath of officer-involved shootings.

"I really enjoy what I do now," John said. "I still feel connected to the brotherhood, but I don't have to do the job. I do not miss the nights or weekends or any of that, but I get to represent the police officers."

John's career has come full circle.

"If I can save one person from going through the shit I went through—save one cop from losing their job, becoming an alcoholic, or losing their marriage—then it's worth it," John said. "My big thing is to encourage officers to ask for help. One of the best things I've done is to talk about it. My chief would've supported me. All I had to do was go in there and ask, but I didn't."

JOSEPH PADILLA

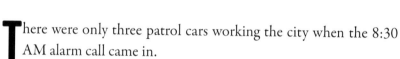

There were only three patrol cars working the city when the 8:30 AM alarm call came in.

Joseph Padilla responded to the jewelry store where the alarm was going off while the other two officers were at a restaurant. They were not excited about breaking to back him on another routine silent alarm at a business.

When Joseph arrived, he started to check the building by shaking the back doors of the jewelry store. He walked around to the front of the business and noticed a man inside, bobbing his head up and down behind display racks as he was moving through the store.

By then, his backup had arrived, and Joseph told him, "I think we've got a janitor in there."

The officers walked in and separated. Almost immediately, a man stepped out from behind a display rack and pointed a gun at Joseph's head.

"I'm going to fucking blow you away," the man yelled, standing only 10 feet away.

"At first, I didn't really take it seriously," Joseph said. "I was so new that I thought this was part of the training process. I didn't know if I could even take my gun out of my holster."

Joseph had been a police officer only for five weeks. The department was small and short staffed, so in those days, he was able to start working patrol before attending the academy, after two weeks of riding with a training officer.

"I got scared as the suspect raised his gun and kept hollering at me," Joseph said. "It was the look in his eyes—that's when I realized it wasn't training, and he was going to kill me. I was 20 years old. I had a wife and baby at home. I was scared shitless, and I wanted to hand in my gun and quit."

In those split seconds, all of those thoughts went through Joseph's mind. Joseph does not remember drawing his gun, nor does he recall how many times he fired. The investigation later showed that Joseph shot twice. One bullet went through the suspect and the second severed the suspect's aorta and lodged in his spine.

"I thought I missed him," Joseph said. "He never flinched— he never did anything. I thought he'd be flying backward like in the movies."

It was not until the man's eyes rolled back into his head that Joseph realized he had shot him. Joseph ran up and ripped the gun from his hands before the suspect dropped to the ground.

It took a moment for Joseph to realize the man he shot was black, but the man he thought was a janitor was white.

"Shit, there's more of them," Joseph thought.

Joseph searched the building and found two hostages lying face-down in an aisle. They were both hog-tied, with their hands and feet tied behind their backs.

The man Joseph saw bobbing his head up and down was actually a hostage. The suspect had tied him up and was forcing him down the aisle. The suspect had taken the two employees at gunpoint while robbing the store of cash and jewelry.

Joseph calmed the hostages down and returned to the suspect, who was still breathing on the floor.

"I was looking down at him and he was just staring at me," Joseph said. "I was alone with him, and I remember those heavy breaths. I looked at him and calmly said, 'You're going to die.' Then he took his last breath. It was the weirdest thing."

After the shooting, Joseph was in a state of shock and did not sleep that night.

"I felt numb for the first day or two," Joseph said. "But then I just assumed that's what cops do—they shoot people and just deal with it."

The department sent Joseph to a police psychologist, and after a brief talk, the doctor felt Joseph was pretty well adjusted, so he returned to work.

"I didn't know how I would be viewed," Joseph said. "When you're a new police officer, you just want to be accepted, but it was really strange, because it was like an unspoken thing. I couldn't really deal with it because nobody talked about it. Nobody ever sat down with me and asked, 'What happened?'"

Joseph felt that everyone at the department was afraid to bring it up because they did not know how he would react as the new kid.

"What bothered me initially," Joseph said, "was that it didn't bother me. When I thought about the shooting, it was just empty— darkness. I felt like I never absorbed it."

About four months later, Joseph went to the police academy, and one of his instructors happened to be the district attorney that had been part of his shooting investigation.

Joseph never mentioned his shooting at the police academy, but the instructor told the class about the incident.

"After that, everybody wanted to hear about it and asked me if I was ok," Joseph said. "That's when it started hitting me that it was an unusual situation."

In the year following his time at the academy, Joseph worked alone on graveyard shifts and thought about the shooting when he approached similar storefronts for alarm calls.

"I kept replaying it in my mind," Joseph said. "I had dreams about it initially, but when it came to dealing with it, I just blocked it out. I didn't want it to affect me, so I just wouldn't deal with it. I don't know if that's healthy or not."

After the shooting, Joseph began feeling isolated, like he no longer fit in at the department. He transferred to a larger agency, where he ended up shooting his weapon three more times during his career.

The second time Joseph shot his weapon was while several officers were pinned down by a suspect shooting a .30-06 rifle at them through gun ports in a trailer.

"When those rounds went past your head, you could just feel the wind zip past you," Joseph said. "It was weird. I'd never felt that before."

A citizen was shot and pinned down in front of them, so Joseph laid down suppression fire while the other officers tried to rescue the man. The SWAT team eventually killed the suspect.

Joseph said his third shooting happened when the driver of a stolen car tried to run him over, but no one was hit.

"It was my fourth shooting that kind of jacked me up," Joseph said. "It was one of the most bizarre things."

Joseph was sitting at his desk, working as a captain in a gang unit, when he heard someone on the radio announce a subject with a gun in the station parking lot. Joseph ran out of the office and into the parking lot.

"My wife was always pissed off at me," Joseph said. "'You get involved in too much stuff' is what she always told me, but I was a cop at heart. When I made captain, I didn't have it in me to just sit in the office."

When Joseph got out to the parking lot, he expected to see officers holding someone at gunpoint during a traffic stop.

"I didn't see anybody," Joseph said, "except for a beautiful woman in tan slacks and a white blouse, with long brown hair. She was holding a Smith & Wesson handgun like mine. I thought she was a detective."

At first she was walking toward Joseph, but then she turned and walked toward some parked cars. She was looking for someone.

"Who's she looking at?" Joseph wondered. "That's when I saw a man trying to dodge behind a car, and she cranked off a couple of rounds."

In fractions of a second, Joseph was flooded with several confusing thoughts.

"Who the hell is this woman?" Joseph had wondered. They had a metro gang task force where officers from multiple agencies were often at their department, but then he recognized the man ducking behind a car.

"I couldn't believe what I had just seen," Joseph said. "The guy ducking was one of my guys. He was out of uniform, but I recognized him. I thought she was a cop, but she lowered the gun and fired at my officer. That's when I pulled my gun and I fired one round at her with my .45."

Joseph said it was a conscious but difficult decision to shoot her.

"It wasn't like where you had these bad guys that looked like bad guys," Joseph said. "You know, gang members, or bikers with guns coming at you—there was none of that. It was somebody's wife."

As soon as Joseph shot her, she took off running and hid behind the off-duty officer's open truck door. Joseph said he has been in two fatal shootings, and in both cases, neither suspect went down after being hit.

Joseph could see the woman crouched behind the truck door, and then he heard a rapid succession of bullets.

"Oh my God, she's killing the officer," Joseph had thought. "I aimed at her right through the door, and I could see the rounds hitting the door. When she hit the ground, she just collapsed like the air was deflated out of a pillow. I'll never forget that."

Joseph ran around the open truck door, and the woman was lying there next to an 80-year-old man.

"Oh my God, I shot an old man that was walking through the park," Joseph had thought. "My heart went through my stomach because I thought I killed an old man."

While Joseph was trying to process shooting the old man, officers ran up and told Joseph that the off-duty officer had also been shot.

"I knelt down, and the old man reached up and grabbed my hand," Joseph said. "He started talking to me, but I couldn't tell what he was saying. The woman was just looking at me and gurgling. They both died right there with me."

Within moments, officers began responding from everywhere and were looking for guidance on how to help with the crime scene.

"They're all coming to me because I was the highest-ranking officer," Joseph said. "I was just in shock. It was hard to process, and nobody realized I had been involved in the shooting. I got ahold of my night-shift lieutenant and said, 'This is yours. I can't deal with it.'"

Joseph went into the gang office and sat there to be alone.

"It was just too much," Joseph said. "My stomach was in my throat, and I had a hard time breathing. I felt guilt about the old man, and shooting a woman was very difficult."

Joseph was taken to headquarters and separated from other officers until the lawyers and investigators arrived. As the investigators sorted things out, they began to learn what had happened.

The old man was having an affair with the 40-year-old woman, who wanted him for money. When their relationship deteriorated, the man served the woman with a restraining order. The woman took him hostage at gunpoint and ordered him to drive until she was ready to kill him.

At the last minute, the man pulled into the police department parking lot and fled behind the off-duty officer's truck. The officer just happened to be there as the situation unfolded.

When Joseph had come out of the station, the woman was looking for the old man, who had fled behind the truck. After Joseph shot her, she ran to the truck and shot the old man multiple times. She hit the off-duty officer, giving him a grazing wound.

None of Joseph's bullets hit the man or the officer, but Joseph did not know that until much later.

"I still feel bad about the whole thing," Joseph said. "I had a lot of anxiety because I wondered if I had shot at her a bunch of times, whether I could have killed her before she got a chance to shoot the old man and the officer."

As the story unfolded, Joseph became more confident that he had made the right decision. The police chief and Joseph's attorney both confirmed that he had done the right thing, which helped relieve some of his anxiety.

Reliving the incident while going through the investigators' interview was difficult, and by the time Joseph got home, he could not sleep. Joseph's stomach was in knots and he felt anxious, so he stayed home for the weekend but returned to work on Monday.

"That first day walking back into the building was like a horror movie," Joseph said. "It was like walking down the hallway with the dark music playing like something's going to happen. That's how it was for me. I wanted out of there because every time I'd pull in the parking lot, I'd relive it."

So after a few months, Joseph transferred to a different division.

The department sent him to a psychologist, but he felt it was something he had to work through on his own.

"I have a hard time going to psychologists," Joseph said. "It's just hard for me to be that guy who sits there and cries for help."

Joseph explained that being a captain kind of isolated him and limited whom he could talk to.

"Some of the best cops I've ever met never took a promotional test," Joseph said. "It takes a different kind of man to keep your street skills sharp for 30 years."

In hindsight, Joseph wished he could have done something more to help himself rather than just not deal with it.

"I think that after we are police officers for a number of years, with what we experience, we become softer inside, but we build a harder shell on the outside to protect it," Joseph said. "I was able to block out that shooting when I was a 20-year-old rookie, but the shooting as a captain really bothered me—it's different being 20 than 50."

Joseph received a medal of honor—the highest honor a police officer can receive—for that shooting, but he is convinced the stress and internal politics of being a police officer take years off of your life.

"What really helps me to this day," Joseph said, "is knowing I did a good job and that I did the right thing."

LOUIS TANORE

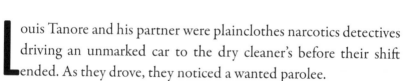

ouis Tanore and his partner were plainclothes narcotics detectives driving an unmarked car to the dry cleaner's before their shift ended. As they drove, they noticed a wanted parolee.

"He was an enforcer, a foot soldier from the Mexican mafia," Louis said. "One time, he had guys tied up in his kitchen while his mother cooked breakfast and pretended she did not notice as he tortured them for money."

Louis called for a patrol unit, and he and his partner followed the car to an apartment, where kids were playing outside.

"He was a bad dude," Louis said. "But he had worked for us in the past, so we figured we'd roll him up and get him to work."

Louis was a veteran narcotics officer, and working informants was a routine part of his job. Most of the gang members knew him by name.

Louis went to the back side of the house, in case the parolee tried to escape out a window. His partner went to the front. As soon as Louis got to the back, he heard things being smashed inside the apartment.

"I could hear that the fight was on, and my partner started yelling for me," Louis said. "I ran around the corner of the house, and a window shattered out at me. I thought the dude was trying to run, but no one came out."

When Louis got to the front door, he saw a woman pulling a small child away from the dining room.

"It was a full-on brawl," Louis said. "They were going for it in the dining room, totally wrapped up punching each other. My partner's as strong as an ox, but he couldn't get control of him."

"He's going for a gun!" Louis' partner yelled. "He's going for it!"

"At the time, I didn't know whether he was going for his own gun or my partner's," Louis said. "But when they spun around, I could see the guy's hand was pulling from his waistband."

The parolee and Louis' partner were wrestling, standing face-to-face, hunched over the dining room table.

"When I saw the parolee's arm coming up, I reached in between them and put my gun against his chest," Louis said. "I don't remember pulling my gun out. I just remember thinking, 'Don't hit my partner.'"

Louis had recently attended training where he had heard that contact shots can cause semiautomatic handgun malfunctions.

"In that split second, I remembered, 'Don't push too hard,'" Louis said. "The moment I touched him with the gun, I remembered, 'Back up. Back up.'"

Louis pulled the trigger and heard a muffled pop. Then his partner yelled.

"Fuck," Louis remembered saying. "I felt instant panic that I shot my partner. I was trying to do whatever I could to not hit him."

The parolee fell on the table for a moment, jumped back up, and said something Louis and his partner could not understand. Then he collapsed to the ground.

"Shit, did I shoot you?" Louis asked his partner.

"I'm fine, I'm fine," his partner said, examining the large scorch mark under his arm. "It's just the muzzle burn."

They held the man at gunpoint, but he did not move. People started coming out of the bedrooms, and then a loud bang came from the back of the apartment.

Louis handcuffed the man and did a quick search, but he did not find any weapons.

It happened so quickly that backup had still not arrived. Louis and his partner left the man on the floor and went room by room to clear the rest of the house. They got to the locked bedroom, where the loud noise had come from.

"My partner kicked in the door," Louis said. "When you talk about adrenaline flowing ... The whole door literally came off the hinges."

The loud bang had come from another man that was hiding in the house. He had smashed through a window to escape.

Louis got on the radio to advise the incoming officers, and then he escorted everyone out of the house while his partner stayed behind to perform CPR.

When backup officers arrived, Louis' partner walked out of the apartment, covered in blood. Louis and his partner were immediately separated and taken to the station.

"I wanted to see him," Louis said. "I knew he was physically okay, but I just wanted to ask if he was all right. It wasn't until later I was able to give him a hug for a couple of seconds at the station."

Their lieutenant was pacing in circles at the station and did not know what to do until the attorneys arrived and decided to do the interviews in the morning.

"I went home, and the first thing I did was crack open a beer," Louis said. "Then there was a knock at the door."

A detective came to the house and wanted the clothes Louis was wearing and a blood sample.

"All right, but I'm on my second beer," Louis warned the detective.

The detective had Louis strip to his underwear. She took his clothes while his brother stood by and made jokes about why she did not also want his underwear. After the detective left, things calmed down.

"It was just surreal," Louis said. "You start thinking, 'Did that really just happen?' I wasn't nervous. I wasn't stressed. I was just kind of numb. I was more worried about my family at that point."

Louis' wife was also a detective and had responded to the shooting scene.

"I hadn't really had a chance to talk to her," Louis said. "Because as soon as it happened, there were always people around. I was worried about her concerns."

When the shooting call first came out, Louis' wife was in the detective bureau with her partner. She did not hear the radio call, so her partner insisted that she get in the car.

"He's flying to get there and hitting bumps while she was wondering what the hell was going on," Louis explained as he remembered her story.

"Why are you driving like an ass?" she had asked. "Slow down."

Louis' wife thought they were responding to another routine shooting. It was not until they got to the scene and saw Louis that she realized it was her husband that had been in a shooting.

"She's a good person to have if you ever get in a shooting," Louis said. "She was very protective."

The next morning, Louis and his wife went to the station for the interview. The police chief was out of state, but he canceled his trip and flew back in the middle of the night. The chief showed up for the interviews, and after a knock on the door, Louis' wife opened it.

"She told the police chief, 'He can't talk to you,'" Louis said. "Then she slammed the door in the chief's face."

The attorneys intervened and allowed the chief to be present.

72

Louis and his wife respected the chief, but she was determined to keep people away from her husband, as she had been instructed to do.

The interview was straightforward.

"I knew I had done the right thing," Louis said. "Without saying the words 'Shoot him,' my partner was telling me to shoot the parolee"

Louis' partner wore a leather holster without retention straps, and Louis later learned that the man was trying to pull at the partner's gun during the fight.

After the interviews, the chief complimented Louis on doing a good job, but he warned Louis not to pay attention to the media.

"It was good to know that he had our back," Louis said. "One of the best things he ever did for us was, about a week later ... asking that I bring my daughter to see him. The shooting was in the paper every day with a different story about how we murdered this guy, and my daughter was really upset."

Louis brought his 13-year-old daughter to the station.

He basically told her, "I'm your dad's boss, and you're going to hear that your dad is a bad person, but he's not. He did everything right. Your dad did a good thing."

"I really appreciated him for doing all that," Louis said.

The shooting investigators interviewed about 75 people, and after two months, Louis was cleared to return to work.

The case eventually went to federal court.

"Back then, the city would fight tooth and nail if officers did nothing wrong," Louis said. "Sometimes they would spend more money fighting it than if they would've settled."

During depositions, Louis and his partner had to meet with the family of the man Louis had shot.

"Sitting across the table from the guy's mother and sister was stressful," Louis said. "We'd take a break, and I wouldn't know what to say."

The attorneys were prepared to confront the female witness with each of the different stories she had told the media and spread around town.

"I honestly believe the family just wanted to know the truth," Louis said. "They were hearing the same stories the witness had been telling the newspapers, but under oath, she gave an honest statement."

The judge dismissed the lawsuit after the depositions.

"The female witness had been lying and getting all the homeboys pumped up," Louis said. "She said the parolee was sitting there eating tacos and we just walked in and shot him."

The narcotics team got several reports from informants that gang members were planning to kill Louis. One informant reported that gang members had been following Louis and his son.

"There were a lot of times when I slept with my AR-15 next to my bed," Louis said. "The kids' bedroom faced the street, and the lower half of the wall was brick, so we had the kids sleep on the floor in case the gang members got stupid and did a drive-by or something."

Their son was 8 and their daughter was 13 at the time.

"We made a game of it and pretended we were camping," Louis said. "My daughter was a little older, and I think she knew, but she didn't say anything for my son's sake. She was kind of upset when she found out about it, but my son thought that happened every day because of what he saw on TV."

There were also nights when the family noticed a suspicious car parked across the street.

"It's always in the back of your mind," Louis said. "Not necessarily just because of the shooting but because of our jobs."

When Louis worked on the FBI task force, he ran into a major gang member that was in custody. The gang member was very close to the man Louis had shot, and he was one of the pallbearers at the funeral.

"I don't hate you or like you," the gang member told Louis. "But I want to know, man to man, what happened."

Louis took the time to explain the whole story of what had led up to the shooting.

"Put it this way," Louis explained to the man. "If one of your homeboys was in a fight with someone and the other guy went after your boy's gun, what are you going do?"

"All right, man, I get it," the gang member said. "I fucking hated you, but now we're good."

The gang member reached out and shook Louis' hand.

STEVE HILL

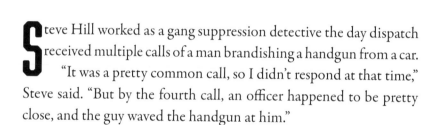

Steve Hill worked as a gang suppression detective the day dispatch received multiple calls of a man brandishing a handgun from a car.

"It was a pretty common call, so I didn't respond at that time," Steve said. "But by the fourth call, an officer happened to be pretty close, and the guy waved the handgun at him."

Steve left the station when the car pursuit began.

"I grabbed my rifle from the trunk and put it on the front seat," Steve said. "I caught up to the pursuit when the suspect fled to the freeway."

While racing down the highway, the driver locked up the brakes and skidded to a stop in the middle of the roadway.

"It's going to go down right here," Steve had thought. "I grabbed my rifle, but then he took off again."

Steve threw his rifle back on the passenger seat, and it slid to the floorboard, almost out of reach.

"I wanted to be able to deploy this thing as soon as I got out of the car," Steve said. "I reached down and picked it up, slung it across my body, and reattached my seatbelt."

Steve drove the car with the rifle muzzle between his legs and the butt stock by his face as he called out the pursuit on the radio. The chase continued out of town, and he began having radio transmission problems. When the pursuit left the freeway for a frontage road, Steve's cell phone rang. It was his supervisor.

"There's a vehicle pursuit of a man with a gun," the supervisor said.

"Um, yeah, I'm number two in the pursuit. I'm calling it," Steve told his boss. "I've got go."

When the pursuit continued onto a small two-lane road, an oncoming driver yielded to the police lights and sirens. The suspect slowed down and stopped next to the citizen that had pulled over. Both drivers sat in their cars, facing each other, a couple of feet apart.

"He's going to shoot the citizen in the other car," Steve had thought. "We're going to have to shoot this guy right here."

Steve put his unmarked detective car in park and started to climb out. When Steve opened the door, the suspect floored the accelerator, so the pursuit continued.

While updating dispatch with his direction of travel, Steve coordinated with the highway patrol to set up a spike strip.

The suspect managed to go around the first spike strip, but the highway patrol set up a second trap on a rural back road, which immediately blew out all four of the suspect's tires. The car began to fishtail and slid to a stop diagonally across the two-lane road.

The first police car hit the spike strip and stopped at an angle behind the suspect's car. Steve swerved away from the spike strip and pulled in next to the police car.

As the suspect got out of his car, Steve stepped out with his left leg, perching his right foot in the doorway of his vehicle.

The suspect had his back to the officers as he fiddled with

something in the door panel. Then he turned to face the officers, who were 20 yards behind.

"I could see it clearly in his hand," Steve said. "He had a Bud Light in his left hand and a black handgun in the other."

The man brought the gun out and raised it toward the officers. Steve aimed his rifle at the man.

"Drop the gun," Steve yelled. "Put your hands up! Put your hands up!"

The next thing Steve noticed was the rifle stock recoiling against his shoulder and the red dot of his Aimpoint weapon sight bouncing around on the target.

"Oh, shit, I'm shooting now," Steve thought. "It was like my body was responding to what I was seeing, but my thoughts hadn't caught up."

Steve focused on driving the sight's red dot to the torso of the man holding the pistol.

"I stopped shooting when he went down," Steve said. "But he didn't fall straight down. When he got hit, he kind of turned and fell to his side."

Without thought, Steve put on his gun's safety and closed the dust cover, just like he had done repeatedly in training. He moved around to the passenger side of his car to check on the officer parked next to him.

"I saw shell casings behind my car," Steve said. "My first thought was that my partner was left-handed, so his gun has got to be fucked up—it should be popping out the other way."

"Hey, are you good?" Steve asked the officer.

"Yeah, I'm good," he answered.

Steve went to the trunk of his car to get a fresh rifle magazine while his partner kept his gun aimed at the suspect.

At the back of his car, Steve ran into one of the new officers and asked if she was ok, but she did not respond.

"I was fucking yelling at her," Steve said. "She did not even shoot, but she had total tunnel vision."

One of the lieutenants walked up and asked who else had shot at the suspect.

"Wait a second. You were shooting behind me?" Steve asked the lieutenant, with a tone of annoyance. "I've seen your shooting on the range!"

The situation was not over. The suspect had fallen into the shrubs on the side of the road, but all the officers could see was his feet sticking out.

They needed to clear the suspect's car to determine if anyone else was in it, and also render first aid if the suspect was still alive.

Steve's plan was to roll his car up to the suspect and use it as cover as he walked forward.

"We can't move the vehicles," the lieutenant said. "This is a crime scene."

"I was fucking livid," Steve said. "It was not a crime scene; it was still an active incident. We could deal with the crime scene later, but we couldn't just let him bleed out and die."

Steve was certain he had shot the suspect, but there was always the possibility the man was lying in the bushes, playing possum, with the gun. After debating with the lieutenant, they waited an hour for the SWAT team to arrive and ended up moving the patrol cars to make room for SWAT's armored vehicle.

Only a handful of SWAT members were available that day, so they needed one more officer to approach the suspect's vehicle. Sending in someone who had just been in the shooting was not an ideal choice, but Steve was the most composed officer on the scene.

"I'm good," Steve told the SWAT sergeant. "This is just business."

Steve was also a SWAT team member, but it was his time playing professional football where he learned how to stay calm under intense pressure.

"I used to do box breathing when I played in the NFL," Steve said. "I take in a breath for five seconds, hold it for five seconds, and let it out for five seconds. A single breathing cycle takes 20 seconds."

Steve consciously took those slow and deliberate breaths during the entire pursuit, and he resumed them after the shooting.

"Okay, dude, relax, take a couple of deep breaths," Steve told himself immediately after the shooting to bring his heartrate down.

Steve walked alongside the armored vehicle, using it as cover, as it slowly crept toward the suspect's car.

"He's still got a gun in his hand," Steve said, remembering that he peered through the suspect's passenger window and through the open door on the driver's side. "He's lying on the ground with blood on him. I can see that rounds went all the way up the side of his face."

For a couple of weeks after the shooting, that scene was the first thought that popped into Steve's mind when he woke up.

"If you were to take a photo of the scene and hold it over my eyes when I woke up, that's what I saw," Steve said. "Every once in a while, I'll still have dreams about seeing the guy lying there after I shot him, but I never had any problems sleeping."

Someone checked the man's pulse even though he was obviously dead, with wounds in his chest and neck, and up the side of his face. The shooting investigators were already on scene and decided to leave the scene untouched.

"Our protocol was to handcuff him, so it was a little awkward leaving a dead guy with a gun in his hand," Steve said. "But we complied and left him there."

After the scene was turned over to the investigators, Steve was taken to a local hotel, where he was given a room to wait for his interview. Steve called his wife and briefly mentioned that he shot someone.

Years later, his wife explained how stressful his career had become for her after the shooting.

"When you don't come home on time, it's a little different now," Steve's wife told him. "When you get called out in the middle of the night for SWAT or K9 stuff, I know it's because someone's hiding or some other bad stuff."

The interview with the shooting investigators went smoothly, until the end.

"When we got done with the interview, a couple of things came up that really bothered me," Steve said. "After the interview, the investigators told me the suspect had a fake gun."

During the investigation, the detectives believed the man had been carrying a real gun, until they went to unload it and discovered it was a replica.

"I knew when it came time for a federal lawsuit, that was going to become an issue," Steve said. "But I thought he came out to engage us in a gunfight, and I eliminated the threat."

The other thing that bothered Steve was when he learned more about the lieutenant that was shooting only a few feet behind him.

"A guy I work with almost killed me," Steve said. "The lieutenant was so stressed out that he didn't even see me standing in front of him. He should have stayed in the lieutenant's office, where his ass belongs."

After about five days of administrative leave, Steve was itching to get back to work.

"I didn't like being off duty. It made me feel like I had done something wrong," Steve said. Before returning to work, Steve had to meet with a psychologist. Steve sat down in the psychologist's waiting room, which was decorated with porcelain dolls.

"This dude had wall-to-wall, floor-to-ceiling zombie clowns and little porcelain china dolls—the kind you see in fucked-up horror movies," Steve said.

"How you doing?" the psychologist asked Steve to get their meeting started.

"I'm going to be honest with you," Steve said. "Your waiting room freaks me out."

"Yeah, I get that a lot," the psychologist said.

"What's your problem, dude?" Steve thought. "That shit freaks me out."

As the conversation progressed, the psychologist asked Steve how he felt about the shooting.

"I felt it was a clean shoot," Steve answered. "I don't want to shoot anyone, but I made peace with the fact that it's something that occurs in my line of work."

"What if the gun turned out to be a toy?" the psychologist asked.

"Then he brought the wrong tool to a gunfight," Steve answered. "What do you want me to say, dude? 'I'm smearing shit on the wall at home'? I'm okay, bro."

Steve felt neither ill will toward the man he shot nor any remorse. Steve later learned the man's wife had committed suicide, and the man had been struggling with a drug problem, but Steve was confident he had responded to the situation exactly as he had been trained to.

Steve reevaluated his training because of the incident. Steve's goal is perfection in training, because he realized performance will always deteriorate under stress.

"I've come terms with what we can actually do under stress," Steve said. "I've heard people say you will rise to the occasion, but that's bullshit. You will only do about 70% as well as you've trained."

During the shooting, Steve shot 10 rounds from about 20 yards away.

"At 20 yards, I can do 10 for 10 all day on a range," Steve said. "If all of those hits from the shooting were mine, I went six for 10. That's 60% at basically panic speed. That was the best I could do at that time."

Even though the shooting was a tactical success, Steve faults himself for not keeping his eye on the suspect after he had gone down.

"I was controlling the gun, trying to drive it to center mass, but when he started to fall, I didn't really track him to the ground," Steve said.

After the shooting, Steve realized that a man lying on the ground, holding a gun, can still be a deadly threat, and that training on static paper targets conditioned him not to follow the target to the ground.

Steve also explained the effect stress has on hearing.

"I distinctly remember hearing radio traffic clearly," Steve said. "People were saying 'Shots fired,' but I don't remember hearing a single gunshot."

Again, Steve likened the experience of the shooting to his time in the NFL.

"You would hear the crowd noise before the snap of the ball," Steve said. "But when you're actually trying to drive, block, and pass block, you never heard the crowd noise. We could talk and communicate with each other, but you don't hear the crowd. I think your mind is able to pick up what you need to hear and block out what you don't."

Steve returned to work, and three years later he was served with a federal lawsuit.

"That kind of stressed me out a little bit," Steve said. "It was all bullshit, but if someone actually believed that stuff, I was going to have some problems."

The lawsuit alleged that the police knew the gun was a toy, but they killed the man because he was Hispanic. The attorneys minimized the significance of the lawsuit and told Steve that he had nothing to worry about because all the evidence supported the officers.

"I was getting federally sued," Steve remembered. "I thought, 'No, this is a big deal.'"

Steve never had to testify in federal court. He filled out a written deposition and the case was dismissed.

TY LEWIS

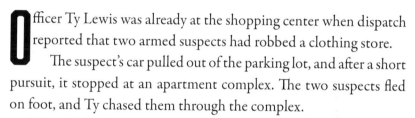

Officer Ty Lewis was already at the shopping center when dispatch reported that two armed suspects had robbed a clothing store.

The suspect's car pulled out of the parking lot, and after a short pursuit, it stopped at an apartment complex. The two suspects fled on foot, and Ty chased them through the complex.

"One of the suspects turned and reached for his waistband," Ty said. "It was a robbery with a gun. Sorry, but I wasn't going to take any chances."

"I vividly remember—it is imprinted in my mind," Ty said. "It's a high-definition picture of his right hand reaching toward his waist as he's starting to look over his shoulder at me. That's the image that replays in my mind when I think about that shooting."

Ty was in a full sprint when he made the decision to pull his Smith & Wesson semiautomatic.

"The only thing I consciously remember is him reaching for a gun," Ty said. "Everything else was on autopilot. I don't even remember unsnapping my triple retention holster. It all goes back to muscle memory and the way we train."

Ty explained how much he had to process in those split seconds while making the difficult decision to shoot the suspect.

Ty had to scan the apartment complex to update dispatch with his direction of travel while watching the suspect reach for his waist-band. Once the suspect made the decision to grab the gun, Ty had to unsnap his holster, draw his gun, and aim, all while sprinting.

"It seemed slower in the moment, but it must have been lightning fast [for me] to perceive and react to all that," Ty said. "I don't know if it's fight or flight, but everything slowed down."

"I didn't feel panic," Ty said. "I felt in control, but when he started reaching and turning, I felt like I had to make a decision before he got the drop on me."

Ty did not have time to focus on his gun's sights during his first shooting. As commonly happens while shooting on the run, the two bullets missed.

The robbery suspects split up, and Ty followed the heavier man, who was closer to him.

"It's like natural selection," Ty said with a laugh. "The predatory instinct tells you to go for the slowest gazelle because you can catch him."

Ty chased him around a corner and blew right past the suspect, who was hiding in an alcove.

"It's scary thinking about it now," Ty said. "I was just flat-out lucky that he wasn't the one with the gun."

Ty arrested him, and the other suspect, who was armed, barricaded himself in a house until the SWAT team later captured him.

Immediately after the shooting, Ty started sorting through the split-second decisions he had made.

"I was a new officer with only three years on," Ty said. "I was apprehensive about what was going to happen."

"It was day shift, so everyone from the chief on down showed up asking me what happened," Ty said. "I felt I did the right thing and I had been treated well, so I told them everything that had happened."

Everyone in the department affirmed that Ty made the right decision. A seasoned sergeant walked Ty through the entire internal affairs investigation without involving an attorney.

"I had a lot of support," Ty said, "and they took care of me."

The investigation cleared Ty, and he returned to work. Ty was confident with his shooting decision, but he explained that his second shooting was a very different experience.

"It makes a huge difference psychologically when you're alone in a shooting than when you're with a group," Ty said. "The group validates that you made the right decision, because everybody perceived the same danger."

Three years after his first shooting, Ty was driving his police car home after a graveyard shift when dispatch advised of a robbery at OfficeMax.

"I've got the suspect's car on Highway 99," one of Ty's partners told dispatch.

The car, a Cadillac, slowed and started to pull over to lure the officer closer, but before it stopped, automatic gunfire erupted out of the rear window. The car accelerated off, and two police cars pursued.

Ty was about a quarter mile away, trying to catch up, when the Cadillac crashed and spun out in an intersection. The first two police cars swerved to avoid the collision as Ty arrived at the intersection.

"I had already made my decision," Ty said. "If this guy gets out of the car with a gun, I'm going to end this right here—brace for impact."

But the Cadillac sped off again, and Ty was now the lead car in the pursuit.

"Back down," one of the officers told Ty on the radio. "That dude's firing a gun."

As soon as Ty heard that radio transmission, a burst of automatic gunfire exploded out of the back window of the Cadillac.

Ty slouched down as low as he could. He chased the car while peering through the gap of the steering wheel, with rounds coming at him.

"I was pissed," Ty said. "I was going to get him no matter what, but I remember thinking, 'Get small or you're going to get hit.'"

The Cadillac sped through a Target shopping center parking lot and high-centered on a concrete planter box. Smoke billowed from the Cadillac's tires as the driver tried desperately to get the car off the planter. Several patrol cars began stacking up on the driver's side of the Cadillac. Ty reached for his shotgun, but it was not there because he hadn't taken his usual car that morning.

"I couldn't see the suspect because the car had dark, tinted windows," Ty said. "I remember seeing muzzle flashes and puffs of gun smoke coming from the back seat."

Ty stood in the doorway of his car and focused his front sight on the muzzle flash.

"I consciously remember taking the first shot," Ty said. "In that moment, I remembered being at the range. We always practiced two things: sight picture and 'press, click, press.' That was going through my mind the whole time."

Ty did not hear the Cadillac's screeching tires or his own gunshots.

"The only thing I remember hearing was 'kaboom' right next to my head," Ty said. "It scared me!"

Another officer had walked up, but Ty had no peripheral vision. The first sound Ty heard during the shootout was the round from his partner's AR-15 leaving the barrel. The second sound he heard was a sergeant yelling, "Cease fire! Cease fire!"

After the shooting, Ty looked himself over to make sure he had not been shot. Another officer looked at Ty's gun belt and pointed out a missing magazine.

"I looked down at an empty magazine on the ground," Ty said. "I had emptied it and loaded another, and I don't recall ever doing that."

Ty fired 24 of the 98 shots the police fired during the gunfight. The suspect had emptied a .357 and a MAC 9 at the officers. After picking up his empty magazine, Ty noticed that several news trucks had followed the pursuit and were filming the shooting live from the sidewalk.

"The first thing that came to mind was that my wife was watching this on TV," Ty said as he choked up and held back tears. "I get a little emotional when I think about my wife watching that unfold."

"I had little ones, you know, so I was nervous," Ty said. "I wanted to call my wife and let her know I was okay."

After Ty called his wife, the shooting investigators brought him to the Cadillac.

"Here was the creepy part about the whole shooting," Ty said. "I remember seeing the back window blown out, and they were in the back seat. The suspect was lying with a MAC 9 in his right hand and an unlit cigarette between the fingers of his other hand."

The shooter sustained multiple gunshots, but the fatal round came from the AR-15 rifle.

"It was gross," Ty said. "One shot went through his temple and had blown his eyeballs out. They were just hanging there."

The female driver was dead, but the female passenger crawled up under the dash and lived.

"Everybody else soaked up the bullets," Ty said. "She ended up surviving and was a great witness."

She later explained that the shooter wanted to lure the cops in to kill them. He wanted to go out in a blaze of glory and take as many cops with him as he could.

Ty had to wait around at the shooting scene for a couple of hours while the investigators sorted things out.

One of Ty's sergeants walked up to him and said, "I couldn't be more proud of you guys. The department and community are going to be proud of you."

"He made us all feel better," Ty said.

Later, back at the police department, the chief walked in with four pizzas and told them, "You guys are part of the legacy of this department now. What you guys did today was heroic and will be remembered. You're all going to be okay."

"That reassurance was huge," Ty said. "His words brought instant reassurance. I had been through it before, but you still have that apprehension about how things are going to unfold."

Having the department's support was the main reason why Ty chose a second time to go through the internal affairs process without an attorney. Investigators took his gun for evidence, but the department gave him another to use while he was put on the standard administrative leave. After the officers gave their statements, everyone began talking about the shooting in the break room, and the typical dark humor began that cops use to cope.

"I really wanted to go home and see my family," Ty said. "My wife had questions, but I didn't really talk about it. I tried to be as stoic as I could and told her it wasn't a big deal. I'm real selective about the stories I tell, and that often irritates my wife, but I don't want her to carry that weight."

Ty spoke about dreams he still has today of weird weapon malfunctions, but the most significant impact of his shootings was how those experiences changed his perspective of the job.

"I don't want to be overly dramatic," Ty said, "but when you're facing a deadly situation and you come out the other side, it changes you. Beforehand, you don't fully appreciate death; you're just doing what you've been trained to do. But when you stop and reflect, it changes the way you approach things and the emotions that run through you when dealing with critical incidents."

WILLY FRANCIS

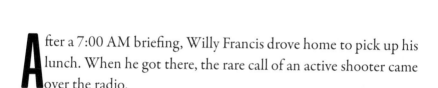

After a 7:00 AM briefing, Willy Francis drove home to pick up his lunch. When he got there, the rare call of an active shooter came over the radio.

"I could hear the 911 phone calls in the background," Willy said. "The phones were going crazy."

Willy flipped on the lights and siren and felt an adrenaline rush as he was blowing through stoplights, racing to the residential neighborhood. Once he arrived and heard gunfire, he felt calm. Another officer was on scene, tending to multiple gunshot victims, so when Willy's partner arrived, they started walking down the street toward the gunfire.

"We had the address, but we had no idea where the shooter was," Willy said. "I heard screaming, and there were victims running everywhere, trying to find cover."

Willy and his partner used parked cars for cover as they walked toward the house. When they got close to the house, the man popped out from behind a six-foot-tall fence.

"He was basically waiting for us," Willy said. "He walked out to the sidewalk, holding a 12 gauge."

Willy and his partner stopped behind a car and ordered the man to drop the weapon.

"I wasn't nervous anymore," Willy said. "I just made my approach like we've practiced time and time again, and when I saw him with the gun, I didn't feel anything."

The man mumbled something they could not understand as he swung the shotgun to his shoulder and aimed it at the ground in front of him.

Willy and his partner raised their voices and added cuss words to their commands.

"I could see the gun clearly," Willy said. "He had his finger on the trigger and started rocking the shotgun toward us. I almost saw the muzzle of the gun."

Willy fired two rounds from his AR-15 rifle, and simultaneously his partner fired two rounds from his Glock handgun.

From 24 yards away, both rifle rounds hit the man in the chest, and one of the handgun rounds struck his hip.

"He was a big boy—about 6'2" and pushing 275 pounds," Willy said. "The 223 rounds went right through him—in and out. It stunned him. He kind of put his gun down a little bit and then pulled back up again."

After the first two shots, time began to slow down for Willy, allowing him what seemed like more time to process things.

"I knew I had made contact when I double-tapped him," Willy said. "You always see in the movies, 'bang,' and then the person falls down. I knew I had him, because I saw his jacket moving when the bullets hit him, but I was concerned when he didn't go down."

Willy did not have time to consciously decide to take the first two shots—they were driven unconsciously by his training and the unfolding incident.

"There was no conscious voice or thought," Willy said. "You just react to how they're acting. You have to get the jump on them, because if you don't, you'll end up like he did."

But after the man raised his weapon a second time, Willy consciously thought about failure drills from his years of SWAT training.

"Everything we did in SWAT was double-tap, headshot," Willy said. "They always teach you to be aware of your background, and I was concerned about the distance. The man was trying to hurt people, but now I was put in the position where I could hurt innocent people in the house behind him."

In those split seconds, Willy consciously decided that he had a better chance of hitting the man's large torso from that distance when compared to the risk of missing the head shot. When the man started raising the shotgun a second time, Willy pressed the trigger.

"I double-tapped him again," Willy said. "He fell with his back facing us, and we couldn't see his shotgun, but I could see his chest rising with each breath."

Seconds after Willy shot the second burst, the police captain arrived on scene, and Willy, his partner, and the captain approached the suspect. The captain asked Willy to handcuff and stay with the suspect. They had no idea if there was more than one shooter, so the captain and Willy's partner left to help the other officers on scene search the house.

"I straddled the suspect and had to use two pairs of handcuffs," Willy said. "When I patted him down, I found 31 rounds of 12 gauge shells. He was ready for war."

As Willy searched the man's ankles, he noticed the impact wounds on his chest.

"The weird part was, when he took his last breath I could actually see the lights turn off in his eyes," Willy said.

Willy felt numb immediately after the shooting, but when his partners began clearing the house, he felt anxiety for their safety.

Police investigators later learned that the whole thing stemmed from a dispute with a neighbor the week before. The neighbor had a bounce house to celebrate a child's birthday, and it blocked the man's driveway. The man was off his medication and stewed on it all week, until he went on a shooting rampage.

After the dust settled, the captain came out of the house and asked who had fired their weapons, but he emphasized that Willy should not provide any details of the shooting.

"I'm really sorry," the captain said when he realized that Willy was one of the officers who had shot the man. "I wouldn't have had you stand by if I had known that."

The captain took the officers' firearms and brought Willy and his partner to the police station, where they were issued new handguns. Then they were taken to a local hotel to wait for their attorneys and the shooting investigators.

"We each got a hotel room, and they took our cell phones so we could not communicate," Willy said. "Then things got a little weird."

When Willy's attorney arrived, they discussed the incident, and the attorney advised him to answer the investigator's questions, but urged him to resist going into a narrative.

Before the interview, the investigators advised Willy of his Miranda rights.

"That was weird," Willy said. "I have never been arrested, so I now was on the other side, but I never felt they were listing me as a suspect. They were very professional and just conducting an investigation."

Willy was not concerned during the interview. He was confident he had done the right thing, and multiple witnesses had seen the man pointing a gun at them. After the interview, Willy went home and sat on his porch with a cigarette.

"It was like a whirlwind," Willy said. "I was getting hit on every side. I was in a haze and could not believe how the day had gone."

Several people called to check on Willy, but he was selective about the calls he answered.

"Some people are more sincere than others," Willy said. "Honestly, instead of a phone call, I'd prefer a text message, just to open the door. That would give me the option to talk."

Willy slept well that night, and when he woke up he was sent to a psychologist. He said that was a waste of time, and two weeks later he was back to work. His partner never returned.

Willy's first radio call when he got back to work was to check on an elderly man with medical problems. When Willy arrived at the man's home, the mail was backed up and newspapers covered the porch. The department was short staffed, so Willy searched the man's home alone.

"The mobile home was really eerie," Willy said. "It was dark and nasty with crunchy drapes."

Willy walked into the bedroom and immediately had to back away and call for someone else to take over.

"That's when it all started clicking," Willy said. "I felt like I was going to have a heart attack. My chest got tight like a rubber band being pulled back."

That was the first time Willy had ever experienced an anxiety attack. Willy was a master rappel instructor for the SWAT team, so he had never been afraid of heights, but "the best way to describe an anxiety attack is like standing on the edge of a building," Willy said. "You've never been afraid of heights, and all of a sudden you're looking down and freaking out."

Willy continued working for a couple of weeks and began having dreams about the shooting.

"It was a vivid, step-by-step replay," Willy said, "like watching a movie and then replaying it again."

In one of the dreams, the shooter's eyes glazed over, and then he came back to life and asked Willy why he had shot him. Willy was sleeping only an hour or two each night, so he started calling in late to work.

"That's when it all started getting real shitty," Willy said.

The department sent him back to the psychologist, and he was put on paid leave.

"The one question that used to piss me off every single time I went to these counselors was 'How does that make you feel?'" Willy said. "How the fuck do you think it makes me feel, and how is that going to make me better?"

Willy explained that it is hard to relate to somebody that has not been in your shoes. Soon the psychologist was prescribing depression medication and dream blockers.

"I tried them for a week, and they made me feel like a zombie," Willy said. "I was kind of numb, and every step I'd take felt like a brick was on my foot. I just couldn't get out of my own way. I had no ambition to do anything, and that's not me. I'm normally go, go, go, all the time."

After a week, Willy trashed all the medications and was never provided an alternative to cope with the PTSD. Instead, he was sent to retake the psych test he had taken when his law enforcement career began.

"I took the 500-question bubble test that asked questions like 'Do you want to be a florist or a race car driver?'" Willy said. "I was told to answer honestly, and I did, but I guess I didn't do so well."

Eight months after the shooting, Willy was let go from the police department, with a stress retirement.

"They said 'See you later,' I retired, and that was it. I was gone," Willy said.

There was no retirement party to honor Willy's years of service, but he was nominated to receive awards for his actions on that day. Willy skipped the awards ceremony.

"I was just doing my job that day," Willy said. "It's just like working as a cashier. We train to do this, and that's what I did."

Willy grew up in the community where he worked, so everyone in town knew about the shooting. One day, Willy was at Walmart with his kids, and some guy walked up to him.

"Hey, you're Willy Francis," the man said. "Damn, I heard you smoked that fool."

Willy's kids were 7 and 5 years old at the time. They were too young to understand, so he had not told them about the shooting.

"The thing that broke my heart was when I walked out of Walmart and my son looked at me, crying," Willy said. "After I checked out, he asked, 'You kill people, Dad?'"

On another occasion, Willy went to have drinks with some friends to celebrate a birthday party. One of the family members of the man Willy had shot was at the bar and confronted Willy.

"Killer motherfucker," the woman screamed. "You piece of shit. How do you live with yourself?"

The woman was kicked out of the bar, but the night was already ruined for Willy, so he went home. These incidents happened everywhere he went in the small community, and he even caught media photographers hiding in bushes outside his house.

"I stopped going anywhere," Willy said. "I was afraid to take my kids anywhere because I was afraid that would happen. They don't need to be part of that. You kind of have to isolate yourself."

Willy never received treatment beyond pills and some counseling, and today he sleeps only four hours on a good night.

"I found that staying busy helps," Willy said. "You just have to find something that preoccupies your mind. If you sit at home and watch TV all day, you can create a lot of bad habits. I know a lot of guys that are retired that drink and smoke bud all day. That's not my thing. I just can't do that."

Willy keeps his mind occupied by exercising and focusing on his kids.

"I run a couple of miles every day and coach my kids' teams to keep busy, but really, you have to come to the realization that you did the right thing," Willy said. "Something can cover it up, but it will always be there. It'll never go away. I will always remember, but as an officer you're given a badge and a gun to uphold the law and keep the community safe. If someone is clearly breaking the law and puts your life in danger, then you have to react."

ABOUT THE AUTHOR

CHUCK RYLANT has been involved with the law enforcement community and use of force training for 20 years. Aside from some business projects, law enforcement and use of force training have been the primary focus of Chuck's entire career.

Chuck began his law enforcement career as a patrol officer and later worked as a detective. He taught firearms and arrest and control (ARCON) at two police agencies and at the police academy. Chuck was a firearms instructor in Las Vegas at Front Sight Firearms Institute, the world's largest firearm training center. He also served on a police SWAT team.

After retiring from law enforcement, Chuck became the lead ARCON instructor at the police academy and he also teaches the train-the-trainer course to officers that come from all over California to become ARCON instructors. Today, Chuck divides his time between teaching, writing, consulting, and use of force expert witness testimony.

Connect with and learn more about the author at
www.ChuckRylant.com.

BONUS MATERIAL

The book you hold in your hands is only the beginning.

There are a ton of FREE articles and additional interviews available only to readers of this book.

As a FREE registered VIP member at www.ChuckRylant.com, you will receive brand-new interviews and other inspiring articles immediately as they are published.

Visit www.ChuckRylant.com and join the VIP list before you get distracted.

Made in the USA
Middletown, DE
02 December 2017